PUBLIC SPEAKING
AND OTHER PLAYS

PRAIRIE PLAY SERIES NO. 31

PUBLIC SPEAKING AND OTHER PLAYS

CHRIS CRADDOCK

NEWEST PRESS

LIBRARY AND ARCHIVES CANADA CATALOGUING IN PUBLICATION

Craddock, Chris, 1972– [Plays. Selections]
Public speaking and other plays / Chris Craddock.

(Prairie play series ; 31) Contents: Public speaking — Porn star — Moving along. ISBN 978-1-927063-45-3 (pbk.)

I. Title. II. Series: Prairie play series ; 31

PS8555.R238A6 2014 C812'.6 C2013-906973-9

Editor for the Board: Anne Nothof
Cover and Interior Design: Natalie Olsen, Kisscut Design
Cover Photo: © Sam Estok
Interior Photos: Public Speaking — photo by Ian Jackson / EPIC photography, Porn Star — photo by Ian Jackson / EPIC photography, Moving Along — photo by Sam Estok

First Edition: March 2014

NeWest Press acknowledges the support of the Canada Council for the Arts, the Alberta Foundation for the Arts, and the Edmonton Arts Council for support of our publishing program. We acknowledge the financial support of the Government of Canada through the Canada Book Fund for our publishing activities.

NeWest Press
#201, 8540–109 Street
Edmonton, Alberta T6G 1E6
780.432.9427
www.newestpress.com

No bison were harmed in the making of this book.

Printed and bound in Canada by Gauvin Press

To Jania and Cal, who are my everything.

CONTENTS

Introduction 9

Public Speaking 11

Porn Star 63

Moving Along 105

Playography 163

Biography 166

INTRODUCTION

Someone is to blame for all this, and I guess that person would be Daniel MacIvor. He came to Edmonton just when I was soaked in all my artistic stem cells, and he did his piece *House* and that was that. His input impressed upon my cells and he accidentally made me an embryonic version of what he was. I would also do solo shows.

I loved the focus, the heroic nature of it, to stand alone against an audience's boredom and hope, and to deliver. This became my dream, and as it was a relatively modest one, it came true early and often, and now look! You're holding a book of them!

And I guess if anyone taught me to do these shows, it was the people who directed them, so I'd like to thank Steve Pirot, my classmate who kicked me around for my first try *SuperEd*,[1] and then Eileen Sproule, who was like an Olympic coach on *Ha!* Sophie Lees first put me through my paces on *Moving Along* and later passed that baton on to Bradley Moss. It was Brad who saw me through *Public Speaking* as well, and as he is my longest-standing collaborator, I will always owe him a debt.

And now I owe you a debt too, my reader. Thanks for finding this book wherever you did, and reading it, maybe all the way through. And if it inspires you to do likewise, I'm glad. There's a lot more solo shows out there these days, and I'm glad about that too. It means there is still courage.

---

1 *SuperEd* is published also by NeWest Press in their first *NextFest Anthology*, and *Ha!* is published by nobody and probably never will be.

DANGEROUS

PUBLIC SPEAKING

PRODUCTION HISTORY

Public Speaking had its world premiere in Edmonton, at Theatre Network, April 21 through May 8, 2011.

Starring: Chris Craddock
Director: Bradley Moss
Set & Media Designer: Paul Bezaire
Lighting Designer: Scott Peters
Sound Designer: Dave Clarke
Costume Designer: Sheena Haug
Stage Manager: Shauna Murphy

Previous to this, *Public Speaking* did a workshop run at the 2010 Toronto Fringe, using the same team as the world premiere, but with Mr. Moss acting as stage manager, and without video projection.

CAST OF CHARACTERS

Patrick Spencer — A bestselling author and motivational speaker
Brian Calhoun — A heroin addict who suffers from gigantism
Diana Spencer — A teenaged girl, addicted to cocaine, sex
Detective Stone — Hardboiled police

NON-SPEAKING
Wing — A community leader
Moose — One of Johnny's thugs

PRODUCTION NOTES

The original production's set was simple: a single chair, with a smaller chair attached to its back. The smaller chair is used for Brian, to suggest his size. Screens for projection were used to project text from Patrick's speeches, as well as fire and other images. A microphone was worn and used with voice modulation to improve voices and add drama when needed. Brian's size was managed through the use of the small chair, and using height differentials amongst characters during dialogue.

Blackout. The performer walks onstage. He speaks in the darkness as Patrick.

Patrick: Public speaking.

It frightens most of you. It terrifies you to your core. Because it is the one time that you know —

He turns on a flashlight and sweeps the crowd. It settles in on someone.

That everyone is looking at YOU.

Your heart rate rises. You try to laugh, act cool, yes, but *inside*, you are just praying for it to stop.

And if the rest of us listen very closely, we can almost hear his thoughts.

The performer switches voices.

Audience Member: This is really uncomfortable. Jesus Christ, what is this? Laugh, I should laugh, this shit happens, ha ha ha ha . . . Fuck. Oh fuck, this is awful.

I wish everyone would stop looking at me.

Patrick puts his flashlight up to his own face. The modulation goes away.

Patrick: It's scary. Being in the public eye. But it doesn't have to be.

Stage lights up.

That's why you're here! Welcome to Dragon-Masters!

We hear inspirational music! He indicates the man in the audience.

Wasn't our friend brave? Give him a hand.

Patrick leads the audience in some applause.

He was brave!

A dramatic sting is heard, taking the music out.

Because everyone was looking at him, and that is scary! But why is it scary? Who are you to be looked at, you ask yourself? But I ask you: Who are you NOT to be looked at? Are you not beautiful? Are you not a unique blending of your unique parents, in a culture, on a planet, hurtling through the cosmos? You are! And that makes you special. Every one of us deserves a good looking at. And none of us need to be afraid when it comes.

And it will come. You will be asked speak out loud in front of people before you die. You'll have to. Society will require it, you may profit from it, the law may *even command it.*

If you are here, now, in your theatre seat, then you have already begun on your life's most important journey. Your path is thorny and dangerous, and contains monsters so fearsome it is as if you designed them in the nightmares of your childhood, and this is because, you did! It is a Hero's journey, and its object is the rescue of an innocent, locked away in a tower lo these many years. The final monster is the most fearsome of all, a great dragon, with claws of guilt! And breath of recrimination! And this disgusting creature currently has full control . . .

He points at his head.

. . . of your head-castle. He lounges within, corpulent and gross, staining your carpets and befouling your tapestries.

What to do? Shall you settle for a lesser life, and leave your head-castle to the dragon who has stolen it? Or will you put on armour and fight for what is yours?

You have chosen. You are here now, so you have chosen to fight!

And when the dragon lies bleeding and the innocent comes blinking into the light, then you will see it was all worth it. Worth ten times ten of what you spent in time and energy and money to get here.

Because the innocent you will rescue is . . . YOURSELF.

So, why not slay the dragon? Hmm? Why not? Why not this very day, slay the dragon of fear that lives in our head-castles?

Why not say, out loud, right now, I will slay the dragon. Come on!

I will slay the dragon.

Say it!

I will slay the dragon.

I will slay the dragon.

Once more!

I WILL SLAY THE DRAGON!!

Dragon: ROAR!

The performer switches to a monster's voice. He roars like a dragon. Fire is suggested. Switches voices again to Brian. He sits in the small seat. He drinks from a tiny mimed cup.

Brian: I guess I'd like to start with an apology. I'm really sorry to Diana, and her father, who I know suffered lots of stress. I myself suffer from an ulcer, so I know that stress has a physical as well as an emotional side. Stress can kill you faster than a gun. If you're a bad shot.

I mean, the last thing I ever wanted to be was a junkie, living in my Dad's old car. My Dad died in that fireworks accident, just two years after Mom had the stroke. And there I was. Being an orphan and a physical freak who never did good at school. I fell into a bad crowd and soon I was doing drugs. I tried everything, but heroin was the one that stuck.

And after I sold the house and dog and the furniture and the fish tanks and the old Sega Genesis videogame system, you know, to get drugs, all I had left was the car. So I'd live in that. It was my Dad's special 1976 Cadillac Calais, and there was no way I was gonna sell it for heroin. You'd think it would be bad, on account of the legroom issue. But I took out the front seats, so it isn't that bad. Nothing's really that bad, provided you're on heroin. You're on heroin, you don't mind stuff as much. Comforts and . . . morality, and all that.

That's not an excuse. But it's a reason.

Of course, you can see the size of me. It's polite of all of you not to mention it, but you must've noticed. It's not normal. See, there's a gland, in my head, the pit-u-itary gland, and it regulates my growth. You got one too, but mine it just keeps going and going. That's why I'm like this. Last time I checked, I was seven feet nine inches, but I know I've grown since then.

So, you can see, my size was all I had going. The only thing that made me special at all. It makes me scary, I know. I look like a fucking monster half the time. It makes people keep their distance — bad people sure, but good people too. Good people especially.

And there's this dealer, Johnny Three Fingers. His name is because he has three fingers on his right hand, they say from grenade shrapnel back in Africa. I buy my medicine from Lil' Charles' corner, but everybody knows Johnny is his boss. We all see his Hummer on the corner, scaring us all with the size of it. I was buying my medicine, but I was fifty cents short. And that was how I met Johnny.

Johnny is smoking on the stoop when he sees Brian. He does a double take and walks up to him, looking way up to his face.

Johnny: How da fuck you stay that big on the tar?

Brian: I dunno. I get hungry. I gotta eat on account of I'm always growing.

Johnny: You mean, you gonna get bigga? Hahaha he gonna get bigger, muthafucka gonna get bigger!

Johnny shares a laugh with his crew. He turns back to Brian.

What's this now, you fifty cents short?

Brian: Yeah. Can you could give me a break? I mean it's only fifty cents.

And I feel everyone stop and then I remember why. I said *only* to Johnny. About money. You see Johnny's from Nigeria, and he was poor in ways Canadians can never understand, even if they're junkies who live in their dad's old car. He once beat a guy to death for saying "only" about five bucks he owed, and this is a famous story where I live. So I really screwed up bad, and Johnny said:

Johnny is still, but then breaks the tension with a laugh.

Johnny: Yeah, I give you a break, Giant Man. I give you your big break.

Johnny leads Brian away. The performer switches to Diana. She sits awkwardly, at her sexual addiction group.

Diana: Hi. My name is Diana.

A Crowd of People: Hi, Diana.

Diana: Hello.

Pause.

I don't wanna say it. I know you all said it, but I don't wanna say: My name is Diana and I'm a sex addict, because I don't know if I am? There are doctors, real psychological doctors who claim there is no such thing and maybe they're right? I'm on their side.

I mean, whatever, my therapist said, and here I am, but I think I'm really here 'cause I'm a girl. I like sex and I'm a girl, so I must be sick. If I was a boy it would be ha ha ha, teenage boys are so horny.

I know that being an emancipated minor like me, I need extra guidance or whatever, or else I risk being a super-fucked-up mega-bitch and I'll spend all this money on coke and be a freak. I don't want that and neither do any of my agents. So I am trying to get healthy and this is the method available. So here I am, going along, with reservations. These reservations stem from my trust issues, which you can feel free to cure while you're in there.

She laughs, but no one joins in. She regards them coolly.

Cuz, this is the cure, right, to sit and speak to you guys? I do wish you luck and all, but seriously, your stories. They're hot. It's seriously, like, titillating, you know. I mean – You and the pool boy? And you, giving blowjobs at the airport? It's torrid! I wasn't doing any of that stuff, but now I kinda want to. This is like treating obesity with ice cream!

She laughs and it becomes awkward again.

You know, 'cause it does the opposite . . .

And maybe I'm cured already, because right now I would love to get high and fuck a dangerous-looking guy that I don't know. It really gets your mind off of stuff, you know, and I would *love to*, you know, but I won't.

And that first step. Admitting that I am powerless? I dunno if that's really true? I feel pretty powerful. Young, rich, famous, I mean that seems like a lot of power. There's a book and movie coming out just based on my real life. I have *offers*.

And number two? That a higher power will return me to sanity? That means God, right? Like a big guy with a white beard who says —

A large bolt of lighting and voice change, to deep and booming.

God: YOU ARE SAVED! Or YOU ARE DAMNED!

Voice change, back to Diana.

Diana: I don't know if God exists, but I know for sure God can't make people not want sex. It doesn't even work on Catholic priests, so . . . how am I supposed to feel? Like my Dad says. It's not my fault. And I don't care anyway.

We rejoin Johnny and Brian, a few minutes later. They walk into Johnny's apartment.

Johnny: Right dis way, Giant Man. Watch your head.

Brian: I was scared. I mean, I was scared of Johnny before I ever met him, and now I was with him, I could see it was good thinking. Johnny wasn't right in the head, you know, or maybe his soul, if you believe in that kind of thing. I was scared to be inside of his apartment, but it was nice in there. I could stand up straight, and he had the biggest TV I ever saw.

Now you know Johnny, he was a crook of all trades, drugs, girls, gambling, and he hit up shops for protection money. Lately he was trying to move into Chinatown. And it was this last thing that I was supposed to help with.

You see, there was this old Chinese guy called Wing. He was the wisest of the old Chinese wise guys, and everybody did what he did. Johnny Three Fingers said that if Wing fell into line, the other shopkeepers would too, like little yellow dominoes, because Johnny was pretty racist for a black guy.

Hearing about Wing made me kinda like him. He reminded me of my Dad. People would ask him for advice too.

Anyway, the thing about Wing, his one weakness maybe, was that he was superstitious. He believed all kinds of old-school Chinese things that are different from what white people think. White people think that Jesus was magic and that's why they protest down at the abortion clinic. Well, Wing believes in demons. And not like demons that have to stay in Hell like white people think, but like demons who infect your dreams and kill your whole family line, you know, like in that Bruce Lee movie! Johnny thought I would make a good demon, because of my size, and because I never went to Chinatown. Cuz, you know, I'm already taller than everybody.

The performer switches to Johnny.

Johnny: Dis mutherfucka Wing! He got da Chinatown wrapped around his pink shorties, and you is just de guy to whip it from his grip, you feel me? I got me a plan, mega brilliant, megawatt like the sun is my mind, big friend, and we put a scare in him dat take the white from his rice no time.

The performer switches to Brian, who is also impressed with Johnny's way of speaking.

Brian: Because that's what he talks like! It takes forever to learn to understand him. It's like crazy African street Chinese, and some people say he cultivated it on purpose, in case the cops ever tapped his phone.

The performer switches to Johnny.

Johnny: So here da plan. We dress you up something crazy, man. Like with de rags and de makeup for you face. I got a girl she make you up with the makeup, til your own mudder be like, who da fuck? Den we get you up in his place late at night and we scare the Jesus from his Bible, you feel me. We scare the God right outa his piss pot! And den Wing be sayin' all over how Johnny Tree Fing got a demon on his side. Johnny be dipping cash and eating spring rolls for free. You do dis, you do it right? You get high all week, mofo. On de Johnny.

The performer switches to Brian.

Brian: Did you get any of that? The last part, you know, that I could get high all week. I mean that is like a lot of heroin, a week's supply, and maybe I could get ahead on my bottle collecting, and then I'd be a week ahead, possibly *forever.* That's like a dream. So, even though I don't want to be a breaking and entering demon, I have to give it a try, right?

It's my dream.

So I go see this girl of Johnny's and she does me up like Hallowe'en, you know, and she puts this kind of head-dress thing on me that makes me even taller, I got rags hanging off me. I think I kinda look like one of the monsters from *The Muppet Show.* And Johnny gave me this old *Star Wars* toy, and it's supposed to make me sound like –

Quick voice switch.

Darth Vader.

He laughs as it switches back.

All put together I'm a scary monster! And I guess to a guy who sincerely believes in demons I would be a heartstopper.

But it gets worse.

Because we get to his place, just before we go in, and Johnny says I gotta *smell* right too because demons are of death and decay. So he takes these really rotten eggs and he breaks them onto my shoulders. I almost fainted, seriously! But it gets worse. Then Johnny opens up this baggie, and it is literally a baggie of human shit! And I begged him not to, but he broke that open and smeared it right on my chest. It was so gross, seriously. So I was not myself when we burst into the room. I was disgusted and disgusting, and as a homeless person, I have a strong stomach for bodily functions.

Anyway, Johnny picks the lock on Wing's door, and we sneak up to his bedroom. We creep into the doorway and I am standing there over his bed. Then Johnny takes out a long string of firecrackers and lights one of them. He lays the whole string at Wing's feet.

We hear a string of firecrackers going off.

And Wing sat up like a shot. He sits right up and is staring. I can see the smell of me hit him and he almost pukes himself right there.

Johnny slaps Wing.

Johnny: Good morning muddafucka. Wake up and smell de demon!

He gestures towards Brian. Brian rears up like a demon, but then speaks in an aside to the audience.

Brian: And now I'm supposed to roar, right? I'm supposed to roar right now. But I got that Darth Vader voice toy on, so as a result, I was kinda thinking of Darth Vader, so when I roared, like accidentally, I said —

We hear Darth Vader Brian.

Luke! I am your father!

We hear regular Brian again.

Which I figure is a dead giveaway right there. Johnny's looking at me and I know I really fucked up. But Wing only speaks like twenty-seven words of English and I think one of them is "father," and another one isn't "Luke." Because when I said that he got even more scared, and I don't what happened to his real father, but maybe it was demon-related.

Johnny gestures magically.

Johnny: I'm a voodoo mutherfucka, muthafucka, and I broke your fortune cookie and brought a demon to your dreams. I am Johnny Tree Fing and you will RESPECT ME!

Johnny refers to Brian.

Brian: And then I'm supposed to roar again, right? And I open my mouth to roar, but then I can taste how I smell. The eggs and the shit, and I just got so disgusted that I threw up. And I had been to the Sally Ann that afternoon, so I had a full stomach of hamburger casserole and I vomited pretty explosively. I got Wing right in his face. All along the wall really, and the chair and even a little bit on Johnny. I felt like I really blew it, but I guess puking is even better then roaring, because Wing starts to scream and scream like a little girl. Johnny smiles and he lights this traffic flare. He lights it and the room is full of glare and smoke and then he pushes me out of there. We're like ninjas with a smoke bomb. We're gone.

They are outside now. Johnny laughs and laughs.

Johnny: That was the bombingest grenade you ever exploded, that throwing up like that, that was some real demon shit like from *The Exorcist!*

Brian: And later, Johnny reaches out the biggest baggie of heroin I ever personally owned. And he says —

Johnny: You did good, my giant friend. You and me we work together now. You my demon mofo. You my demon forever.

Johnny holds out a bag of heroin. The performer switches to Brian. He gazes at the drugs longingly.

Brian: That's a scary idea right there. I probably should have been scared by that. But all I could see was that bag of heroin. I was a whole week ahead.

He reaches out and takes the baggie. The performer switches to Patrick, still giving his seminar.

Patrick: As many of my fans know, before my awakening, I was a humble public speaking instructor. I observed people as they stepped from their regular lives and into the life of a public speaker. The light of attention came upon them, and instead of embracing its warmth, they would crumble, cringe, and shrink from that glow. And all the while, one question rings in their ears.

What do these people want from me?

The answer is clear. They want what they were promised. And what were they promised? They were promised something that means something to them. You made a promise, and we are taught from a young age that to break your promise is a bad, bad thing. To break your promise is such a bad thing that we would rather freeze immobile, urinate in our pants, drip buckets of ice-cold flop sweat than risk such an outcome.

But I ask you now, is breaking a promise really such a big deal? Especially when such promises and much bigger ones are made and broken every second of every day of our lives? Snap your fingers right now.

He snaps his fingers rhythmically.

In the time it took to make that sound, a solemn vow to a wife, son, brother, or electorate is broken — not just once, but many hundreds of times.

And what about you? You have made promises. Have you not? We all exist in a matrix of promises, and not all of them are kept. This is disappointing, but a part of life. Sooner or later, we fail.

All of you, think of a time when you have failed. Consider it deeply. Really think of it. Imagine. All of you close your eyes, close your eyes, close, close, and imagine a piece of paper, and the story of that failure is written upon it. See the words, see them on the paper, the names, what happened. Everything. Now crumple it! Crumple that piece of paper and throw it into the furnace of forgiveness. FOR THAT IS WHERE IT GOES!

He crumples a mimed piece of paper and throws it into the furnace. A burst of flame is heard, and a fireball appears in the video.

The furnace will forgive you, it will eat your secrets leaving only ash. Leaving only you, reborn.

Once the furnace forgives you, you will no longer fear failure of any kind. When the furnace forgives you, you climb into your head-castle, and you slay the dragon that lives there. When you slay the dragon, it changes everything. You can live in there now. You couldn't before, there was a dragon! But now it's safe and comfortable to do so, and your head-castle can become your home, your fortress, your womb, where you alone matter and where all others are secondary.

Well, I brought these ideas into my life as a public speaking instructor, and they changed my practice profoundly. Soon, I was teaching the philosophy behind my methods more than I was teaching the methods themselves. And this was when, as some say, I became "dangerous."

To this I say, "*Yes*."

I am dangerous, and I wish to be. Dangerous to the stale middle-of-the-road that is the life of the modern human. I wish to breed a generation of futuristic warriors, who live up this life hungrily and greedily, as we were meant to live it! *Why?* Why? Why are we sitting in cubicles, flushing the hours of our lives down some corporate toilet, and not even reaping the rewards! Instead our toil goes to wives and husbands and daughters and charities and relatives who are down on their luck, and other such parasites who would drag you down and keep you from your truest self.

They will pull you under. It is *you* or *them*.

Some do say, "Is all this required?" I mean, it's only public speaking. Public speaking is more than it seems, I think. It's significant. When someone speaks in public, they speak for more than themselves, they enter the public discourse and become a part of history.

Are you ready to be a part of history?

In my small way, I am a part of history, and as such I earn a startling amount of money. But could I have achieved this, if I carried around the many failures of my youth? My alcoholism, my broken marriage, my spoiled daughter, these bother me not at all. The story has been written, you see, and then crumpled up, and then burned in the furnace of forgiveness.

You all have paper and pencils. We'll wait. Write it all down! We'll wait! And prepare to forgive yourself.

The performer changes to Brian.

Brian: My life changed a lot after that. Johnny gave me a secure place to park my car, and sometimes he let me use the shower. He took me to the Big and Tall, and got me this suit, and a long black leather coat. He said I looked badass, and I thought so too.

I also got these fighting lessons from Moose. Mostly, I learned to grab people by the throat and push them against a wall really hard. Which is one of the main moves in intimidation visits. I'd say I use that move more than any others. My hand can wrap around a person's whole neck. They just about poop their pants. Then Johnny talks tough —

Johnny: Talking tough!

Brian: — And then he gets what he wants.

Sometimes, I don't even do anything. I just stare down at the people, with my head up at their ceiling. Just staring, like I'm mad at them.

He does his mean look.

And they get real scared.

Sometimes, I feel pretty bad about it. Sometimes it seems like the people are too normal, and by normal in this case I mean nice. They seem like nice enough people, you know. But whenever I'd feel like that, I'd just get high some more.

At this point I realized that I was turning into an actual criminal. Like a professional, career criminal. And I wasn't real proud of that, but I also knew it was one of the only classes of people who can get high almost all the time.

Pretty soon after that, we heard about Diana.

The performer switches to Diana.

Diana: I guess if I were to be like, one thousand percent honest with you, my sex life was getting kind of dicey. Like, if that's what you mean by being a harmful addiction, I guess you could argue a point. I was getting into some stuff with some questionable dudes. A certain questionable dude.

Okay, this is confidential, right, 'cause I signed exclusivity . . .

People seem eager to hear, so Diana leans in conspiratorially.

And so I started seeing this guy that I bought coke from. His name was Li'l Charles.

It was a misnomer.

She holds her hands apart to imply Charles was well-endowed.

And he was beautiful. So slim and muscled and he had a scar on his chin. That's the adventure scar and I know this because Indiana Jones has one.

And everything would have been fine, except I wanted to go to his place. He liked it at my place for obvious reasons, but I specifically wanted to fuck at his place in the ghetto because I thought it would be hotter. And as I say this, I guess I can see how being a sex addict, or at least a committed sex *enthusiast*, put me at risk. So, good for you!

But it worked, though! Seriously, I'd get so turned on. We'd get down on the mattress on his floor and fuck like we were in the Olympics. Afterwards Li'l Charles would say:

Li'l Charles: I can't believe your father is Patrick Spencer.

Diana: And I'd say I know. I know.

And I get that maybe he bragged about me, about like, bagging this rich girl, and that's why people knew about it, but I don't believe he was in on it. I don't know what really happened in that room.

But I saw there was this gun and a cloth over my mouth, and . . . I just passed out.

The performer switches to Brian.

Brian: So. We were at Johnny's place and I was making banana pancakes for everybody. Me and Moose and Johnny and some girls that were there. I can't really cook, but I can make banana pancakes and spaghetti sauce, and chili, which is basically just spaghetti sauce with beans. I was cooking the pancakes and Johnny came in and he tells us that he heard Li'l Charles had a rich girlfriend and that we were gonna boost her for ransom.

Johnny speaks casually.

Johnny: We gonna boost her, for da ransom.

Brian: Just said it, just like that, like it was a staff meeting! I could hardly believe it. I'm looking around and the guys are nodding. But I guess it was like anything else we did. We did terrible illegal stuff all the time. I mean, we were criminals. It was our job.

And sometimes it's part of your job to not care about things, right?

Anyway, we burst into the room, and they were makin' sex in there. I felt bad, not only to interrupt, but that she was all naked. I felt like she'd be pretty vulnerable-feeling. The only thing worse than getting kidnapped, I bet, is to get kidnapped naked. Johnny held a gun on Charles, and he put a cloth over the girl's mouth and she passed out, and I grabbed up the sheets and the passed-out girl and kinda wrapped her up. I figured she could wear that and that way I wouldn't be touching a naked girl, which you can't do without permission. I ran out of the building and to the van.

She looked so small. Johnny said her dad was the King of Self-help. I guess that made her the princess. The

Princess of Helping Yourself. That was, I think "ironic"? Because she couldn't help herself at all, all knocked out and kidnapped by a giant.

Brian closes the door to the van. The performer switches to Diana.

Diana: So I know it's a cliché in therapy for people to blame their parents for everything, but I do think it's significant that my Mom was suicidally depressed, and my Dad never cared about me. So, imagine me as a kid, with this depressed Mom. And my Dad was a drunk. I mean, can I judge, now, with my coke thing, but honestly, it *wasn't even that bad.* My drunk Dad would at least *try.* But then one day he changed.

He came home early, and he wasn't drunk. He made a pot of coffee, and set up the old electric typewriter and just started pounding on it.

And it turned out, he was writing the book. That first big book.

Am I talking too much? Is it weird? Like, when a famous person talks about a big thing from the media, is that weird, or just like awesome? I assume, awesome.

Diana receives confirmation that it is indeed awesome.

Okay! So all of a sudden my Dad was this different guy. He didn't care, and surprise! It turns out it's better to be drunk and to care than to be sober and not. He didn't hold Mom anymore and he never told me he loved me.

There was one morning he tried to lay it out, tried to explain to us why he was right to treat us like this. Mom sat up in bed and said, "That is the worst thing I ever heard."

And he left.

Then it was me and my Mom. Mom got out of bed long enough to get us some welfare, and I babysat after school. After about two years, we started to see Dad on TV all the time. His book was a major big deal, so I suggested to Mom that it might be a good time to finalize that divorce. She got out of bed, and we dragged Dad to court, and that did not go well for him, you know, for obvious reasons.

That judge threw the book at Dad, and we got a cash settlement that would curl your fucking hair. I had no idea. I really thought that this meant we had won, and probably Mom would get help, and be way better.

But that is not what happened at all. Mom went to get the money from the lawyer and she made up a will at the same time. Then she bought a used car with cash and she uh . . . she drove it off a cliff.

I think she was staying for me, and now that we had money, I was taken care of, she thought. I was taken care of and she was free to go. So she did.

But it turns out she was wrong. My money went into a trust fund, and I went to live with my Dad in his mansion.

I guess I probably could have been an emancipated minor or whatever. But I wanted to try my Dad on for size, see if we could get along. I knew he knew he didn't care exactly, but I thought we could at least be friendly. But he was so busy being the king of self-help that I was left alone to be this weird princess. The princess of being alone in that . . . castle. The princess of registering myself for high school. The princess of helping myself.

Wow. Therapy feels good, right?

The performer switches to Patrick.

Patrick: Sometimes people ask me, how did I . . . become me? What happened to change my thinking so radically from the mainstream? I'll tell you what happened.

I looked into the abyss, and the abyss looked back into me.

I was a drunk, you see, a true alcoholic, throwing my life away in a series of seedy bars, a failure by any definition of the term. My marriage was a disaster of seething resentment and disappointment. My wife was an anchor, sinking the wrecked ship that was our life. My daughter was livid in her adolescent rage, blaming and accusing me with every look. My small business, getting steadily smaller, down to a few straggling pupils, too shy, or loyal, or emotionally stunted to notice that their teacher was an inveterate degenerate. I was trapped in a cage, with every monster that ever plagued me, and my only comfort was a steady supply of my drug of choice.

On the fateful night, I was sitting in a bar, as usual. And as usual, my thoughts were full of monsters. I was thinking:

Why? Why can't I stop drinking? Why can't I do it for my family? Why can't I stop drinking for them?

Was I a terrible person?

Or are these the wrong questions?

Was my responsibility to them a reason not to drink, or was it the very reason I drank in the first place? And the lights went on! I finally knew why I drank. I drank because I was not living for myself. The tension of living in servitude to *other people*, why, it tore at my very soul, and my only comfort was an anesthetic.

I mumbled it at first, the phrase which would become famous. I repeated it to myself with growing strength, until I was shouting it, right in the bar.

IT'S NOT MY FAULT!

People stared.

AND I DON'T CARE ANYWAY!

He tips the chair over defiantly.

It's not my fault, and I don't care anyway.

You've heard it before, you've seen the T-shirts, which are, of course, for sale in the lobby. Its meaning is clear on the surface, but let's examine it in detail. Let's start with the first part. It's not my fault. Let's apply that to something big and disastrous, like say, I don't know: climate change. Climate change is not your fault.

I mean, we are North Americans, we are the leading producers of carbon on earth, but we share that responsibility with hundreds of millions of people. Responsibility sufficiently shared is no responsibility at all. Now, consider a firing squad. It was the practice in firing squads to give some soldiers blanks. That way, no one knew which of them delivered the killing bullet, and thus they *all* evaded the guilt of responsibility. Look how quickly we have moved. From hundreds of millions to a mere dozen! And let's go further, even if it is perhaps, somewhat, "your fault," well, who are you? Are you not the product of your parents, with their flawed genetics, their horrible neglect or their invasive monitoring or some combination of the two? Are you not the person they made you to be?

Yes, you are. You had no choice. Therefore, it is quite simply Not. Your. Fault.

And now the second part. "I don't care anyway."

Now this is trickier. Apply it to climate change, and OH! I can see you already prickling in your seats. Of course you care! You care. You care about the polar bears, you care about Tuvalu, Maldives and the Philippines and all the not-white people thousands of miles away. You *care!* You think. You don't do anything, really, you aren't changing your life per se, you're not really even voting for change, rather against it really, but don't tell me that you don't care, because you do. You do care. Well. To that I ask: Do you? Really? Do you really? Really? Really?

I submit to you, that you don't care. That society changed, at some point, and we simply stopped caring. The change has come, and no one knows why. Was it the media, was it horror movies, was it violent videogames that hardened all our hearts? No one knows. But one thing is certain: It wasn't my fault, and I don't care anyway.

And neither do you.

So say it. Everyone! All together now!

Patrick encourages the audience to chant along with him.

It's not my fault, and I don't care anyway!

It's not my fault, and I don't care anyway!

It's not my fault, and I don't care anyway!

And take your paper!

And crumple your paper!

And say it to the paper!

And throw it into the furnace of forgiveness!

Why not? It's not your fault.

Whispers.

And you don't care anyway.

He throws the paper. Fire comes up and the stage falls to blackout.

Diana: Hello? Hello?

We hear the banging of blindly searching. There is a small light under the chair. She turns it on.

Hello? Is anyone there?

Brian speaks from the darkness. The performer stays Diana and speaks Brian's lines.

Brian: I'm here.

Diana: Hi.

Brian: Hi. You're Diana, right?

Diana: Yeah. What's your name?

Brian: Johnny says I'm not supposed to say.

Diana: That's not very sociable.

Brian: They call me Giant Man.

Diana: You're the one that carried me.

Brian: Sorry.

Pause.

Diana: So I'm kidnapped, right? Like, this isn't a game or a prank? I am actually seriously kidnapped?

Brian: I think so.

Diana: What kinda ransom you hoping for?

Brian: I dunno. A lotta money, I guess. Your Dad is the guy from the TV, right? With the infomercials?

Diana: That's him.

Brian: Johnny showed me a magazine that said he was the 500th richest man in Canada.

Diana: He steals money from stupid people.

Brian: You don't like him?

Diana: I'm a teenager. He's my father. It's complicated.

They switch.

Brian: Well. You're lucky to have a father.

Pause.

Diana: So what happens now?

Brian: I need your Dad's phone number. Johnny wants to call him.

Diana: Okay. (905) 470-8735. Who's Johnny?

Brian: How do you know — shit, I been saying his name. Stupid, stupid, stupid —

Diana: I won't say anything. Promise!

Brian: Stupid — Really?

Diana: Sure.

Brian: Because I'm new at all this, and I don't wanna get fired.

Diana: I won't say anything. I promise.

Brian: Okay. Thanks. Thank you.

Diana: But you have to do something for me. Okay? That's fair, right?

Brian: I guess.

They switch again.

Diana: Well, being a kidnapped person is pretty dicey situation. People get killed, right? It happens all the time.

Brian: You'll be okay.

Diana: It happens all the time. I just want you to look out for me a little bit, okay? I don't want to get hurt or killed or anything. I got money of my own to make it worth your while. You get me through this, and I'll pay you, like, tons. More than these guys ever would. I promise.

So, would you look out for me a little bit, Giant Man?

They switch again.

Brian: Yeah. I would've anyway.

Diana: Thank you.

Brian: Sure.

Pause.

Diana: Can I have some clothes?

Brian: Yeah. Yeah, for sure! Of course. No clothes! Terrible.

Brian runs off, muttering, to get Diana something to wear.

Patrick: Who are you, really? You are this.

He points to his head.

You are this, and only this mass of wiring we call our brains. Where did they come from, these amazing cognitive processors? Well, a simple answer is: they came from the past. They came from parents and grandparents and great-great-grandparents and so forth, back into prehistory. And physically, they haven't changed much since then. And while society transforms itself at lightning speed, we still use the same brains that discovered fire. And we think that we are living as we should, while prehistoric conditions still dominate us.

It begs the question: can one, by the force of their will, evolve?

For example, in the magazines we see women exclaiming, "Why can't men be faithful?" Some know as we do, that prehistoric man was programmed to spread their seed far and wide so that their genetic line may be passed on. Society can say, "Well, change! Be better!" And though it is contrary to men's deepest programming, some can do it. Millions do, for some of the time, all the time.

One can evolve. But are there other, less desirable things that we need to evolve away from? I submit to you, that "compassion" is one of those things. That "concern for others" is merely leftover programming from a caveman era.

Consider:

We see a stranger shot with a loud gun. Do we rush to his side, or do we run screaming? We run screaming. If someone vomits, we wish to vomit too. Is this because it is disgusting? Partially. But partially, it is because your caveman brain warns you that if that person ate something poisonous, you may have eaten it too. That is why you wish to vomit. Not solidarity, but self-interest.

The idea of compassion is the idea that holds you back from being your truest self. It is the shackle that keeps you locked in a life that is based on *other people*. And it keeps your life from being truly your own. This is why we do not do what we dream, we don't climb Everest, we don't write the great Canadian novel, we do not even progress at work. We become old and fat and silly, smiling down at children who are about to tell us to fuck ourselves.

Why?

Love. Compassion. These words that resonate as basically synonymous with virtue, are the very rocks that we put in our pockets to drown ourselves with. Those who do not care, are the ones who go furthest, do the most.

Because they are free!

And I know that this is true. Not only because I feel it to be true in my very bones, but because my truth was tested, and it was borne out.

My time in the desert started with a phone call.

A phone rings.

Hello?

Johnny: It's eleven o'clock muddafucka. Do you know where your daughter is?

Patrick: Excuse me?

Johnny: No you don't. I got her here with me.

Patrick: I'm sorry, who is this?

Johnny: I am the guy who has your daughter muddafucka, and I ain't givin' her back for gratis.

Patrick: I can honestly barely understand you.

Diana: Daddy?

Patrick: Diana, what on earth is going on here? Where are you?

Diana: I'm kidnapped, Daddy! They got me here and they want money before they let me go.

Patrick: Kidnapped? For the love of God, Diana –

Diana: Daddy, I know I've lied to you before, but this is no lie, Daddy! They're serious and they have me and they want money!

Patrick: How much money?

Diana: They want . . . ten million dollars, Daddy.

Patrick turns to the crowd.

Patrick: Now, ten million dollars is a lot of money. But it was also an amount I had. In those days I worried about upheaval in the banks and so I kept cash. The fact was I had exactly twelve million dollars in a duffel bag in the floor safe under the pool table in the basement. I could have gone downstairs right then and gotten it.

Now, what to do? Part of me, of course, the prehistoric part of me, said, "Fix This! You have the power. Get your daughter back!"

I took a breath and divided myself from my prehistoric mind. I sat in my head-castle's most comfortable chair, and I applied my credo.

Was this my fault?

Well, no, surely. This was the fault of the villain on the phone, but also the fault of my daughter. Who I knew was running wild, doing drugs, I knew this.

But back to me, I am the active participant here.

And due to my training in clear thinking, I spied in this . . . an opportunity!

You see, there are many people like myself. People who claim to have wisdom, who claim to follow that wisdom themselves. But how many of them have the chance to prove it? How many of them are blessed with the opportunity to show that they have followed their philosophy to the utmost, and even in extreme cases, they are in indeed as they say they are. I had money, yes, I was well known, sure, but I lacked true fame, and now I had this chance to take my place in the firmament with Deepak Chopra, Wayne Dyer, possibly even further, to the level of a Dr. Phil, or even . . . an Oprah.

Diana: Daddy, please! I know we don't get along right now, I know I haven't been the best daughter, but I am still your daughter, aren't I? I'm your little girl.

She starts to cry.

I'm still your little girl, aren't I?

Patrick turns to the crowd.

Patrick: She said this, and oh did my prehistoric brain kick up a fuss, and I very nearly lost my resolve. But then I remembered the three tenets of clear-think: logic, blame and . . .

He breathes out heavily.

. . . release! And I steeled myself. It's funny now to think, the moment I abandoned my daughter was one of the proudest of my life. And I said:

He turns back to the phone.

Let me speak to the gentleman.

Johnny: You are listening now? I want da money in a black suitcase with wheels. I want it in da trunk of a Lincoln Navigator, also black, brand new. I want da car parked, by you —

Patrick: Excuse me, let me stop you there. You see, my daughter is not quite grown, but she has been behaving as such for years. She does cocaine on a regular basis and spends time with the worst sort of people. Now I will call the police, because that is what a citizen does when he hears of a crime, but I will not pay you. I simply will not.

Johnny: What? No! No police! No police or the girl dies.

Patrick: Yes, that is what kidnappers say, isn't it? But there will be police, and there will be no money, and if you in fact are not some friend of my daughter's looking for more cocaine, well then your choices are your own. But hopefully you can tell by my tone that my daughter and I are not close, and threats against her safety do not have the usual effect.

And then I hung up the phone. And I called the police.

The performer transforms to Brian, bringing Diana clothes. He finds Diana upset.

Brian: I got you these clothes. It's a sweatsuit.

Diana: Thanks. Can you turn around?

Brian: Sure. Does it fit okay? I thought it looked comfortable.

Diana: Yeah, I was pretty uncomfortable before, but now that I have snuggly pants, this situation is just fine.

Brian: It's all I can do.

Diana: He's not gonna pay! Because of his philosophy. This isn't his fault, and he just — He just doesn't care.

Diana starts to cry.

Brian: Come on now.

Diana: He doesn't care! On *purpose!* But I always thought that he'd look after me in the end, you know, if the chips were down, he'd take an interest. I know he has the money. *He has eleven and a half million dollars under the pool table!* But now the chips are down, they are down right now, I am in mortal fucking danger and he just doesn't care. He never cared.

Brian: Maybe he thinks the police are a better option, you know. There's this Mel Gibson movie called *Ransom* and he did something kind of similar. Yeah, he's probably just using his big rich person brain to think of a great new way to save you.

Diana: I would really like to believe that.

Pause. Diana looks at Brian searchingly. She unzips the top of the sweatsuit a little and throws a hip to one side.

Diana: Um, listen. I don't know how into . . . sex . . . you might be, but if it would help, like, at all, we could –

Brian: What?

Brian's confusion turns to fluster.

NO! No. Nononono. No. That wouldn't be right at all – No. No. Thank you. Uh . . .

Awkward pause.

Let's just be *friends.*

Diana: Okay.

She is embarrassed. She awkwardly dresses and tries another tactic.

Okay. So, we need to get to know each other. It's easy. It only takes three questions.

Brian: Okay . . .

Diana: What's the best thing that ever happened to you?

Brian: Jeez, I dunno. Not that many good things happen to me.

Diana: There must be something.

Brian: Um, well, there was this one time. I was a kid and me and my folks were driving around Ontario and we splurged on a day at Canada's Wonderland. You know Canada's Wonderland?

Diana: Sure.

Brian: And I was only four or so, but I was tall enough I could go on any ride I wanted. I saw other kids my age, and they couldn't ride anything. They would come up to the signs that said you had to be this tall and they weren't that tall. For me it was easy.

Diana: That sounds nice.

Brian: Yeah. Yeah. It was a nice day.

Diana: And what's the worst thing that ever happened to you?

Brian: I dunno. It's hard to think of things.

Diana: I know I'm being nosy, but I might not have that much time.

Brian: I guess the worst was when my Mom died. She had a stroke and she was in the hospital, and they were keeping her alive on machines, but she didn't have any brain functioning, they said.

Diana: I'm sorry.

Brian: Yeah. Thanks. But my Mom was the generous type, you know, so she had signed up to be an organ donor. So the doctors knew this, and they started in on my Dad about when we could get some of her organs for other people.

And Dad had this little flashlight, and he would open her eyes and shine the light in, you know? Because if her pupils reacted to the light, it meant her brain maybe had a bit of functioning and maybe she wouldn't have to die after all. So my Dad would do this every so often, just to check for himself. And we had been to the cafeteria, and talk, you know, man to man about letting her go to heaven even though we miss her. And then we went back upstairs to Mom. And she had the prettiest blue eyes. And she never needed glasses, even when she was in her forties. But Dad went to check her eyes with his flashlight one last time, and — they had taken her eyes. They had already taken her eyes.

Diana: That's awful.

Brian: Yeah. Yeah. And I saw my Dad see that and I guess that's the worst thing that ever happened to me.

Diana: I lost my Mom too.

Brian: It's hard, right?

Diana: Yeah.

Pause. Diana is overcome.

Sorry. Okay. Last question. What's your dream?

Brian: My dream? Come on, I'm homeless!

Diana: Even still.

Brian: Well. Well, I was at the library on the internet a while back. And I read something about Holland.

Diana: Holland.

Brian: Holland. It's a country. You heard of Holland?

Diana: Sure.

Brian: Well, in Holland people are very tall. They're so tall in Holland that they recently changed standards for construction and that. Doors are higher there, and the buildings they make are just for taller people, in general. I'd still be tall for there, but I'd fit in a little more, don't you think?

Diana: Sure.

Brian: So I guess if I have a dream, it's that. To maybe go there, and maybe get to live there and maybe . . . not be such a freak.

Diana: I think it's a great dream.

Diana reaches her hand out to Brian and he takes it.

Brian: And I guess right there. Right there is when we became *friends*. And then Johnny came in.

Johnny: Your father a real hardass for a rich man.

He sees what Diana is wearing.

Is dat my Sean John sweatsuit?

Brian: Sorry, Johnny, she was naked and all –

Johnny: Did you just say my fuckin' name?

Brian: Sorry, Johnny – Sorry, Joh – Oh I'm sorry – Sorry!

Johnny: Shut de fuck up. And you little girl. You tink about your least favourite finger. You count 'em all up, and you figure which one you can do witout. Den you write down your Daddy's mailing address.

The performer transforms to Detective Jeremiah Stone.

Detective Stone: So, let me see, I got the call late on Tuesday the twenty-seventh, it was just after eleven, I believe. It was the father of the victim, one Patrick Spencer. I had heard of him, sure, we all us at the station heard of him. He was the Tony Robbins of Canada, right? World-famous for selling those books on how to be an asshole. But at the same time, I felt for him too. I mean, I got two girls at college, and the thought of them being abducted, well, I felt for the guy right away. I grab Smitty and a couple of unis and I headed over to his place. His fucking mansion, I should say — Fuck, I should swear less. Ha ha, Ah, fuck it. It *was* a fucking mansion. In fact, it was a big-ass, fucktown superhouse, I mean, I knew you could get rich doing this stuff he did, but I had no fucking idea.

Anyhow, the guy, Mr. Spencer, he was calm. He was cool as a cucumber margarita, and he lays it all out. He told me that they called, he confirms his daughter was with them, and that he told the kidnapper he was calling the cops. Right there, that's weird. I mean, sure, you call the cops, but you don't tell the fucking kidnapper that you're calling the cops. You tell the kidnapper you would never call any cops, and you'll pay right away, yes sir, no sir, three bags full. Then he tells me he has the money, like, on hand. He's got more than the ransom in a duffel bag right now, right in the house. And the way he's telling me this, I feel like he's proud. He somehow proud of himself for being calm, for screwing up the procedure, for having the money, on hand! And not even trying to offer it.

I tell him, "Sir," and I wouldn't normally tell a vic this, but with the way he's acting, and maybe I'm so close to retirement and I don't give a fuck, but I tell him, I say, "Sir, your daughter might *die* because of how you handled things." And you know what he says to me?

He says: It's not my fault. And I don't care anyway.

He opens his mouth in mock shock, which he waves away.

Detective Stone: I read his books later, so I know where it comes from now. But at the time, it blew my mind. I thought about my girls and all my sympathy for this rich motherfucker went right out the window. I was thinking: Fuck him.

Brian: Oooooooooh! Johnny was mad! Dianna's Dad said he wouldn't pay, so Johnny said that we had to take it up a notch. That made me scared.

They made me put a bag over Diana's head, I think to help me be mean to her. I think Johnny thought I was losing my bad-assness, being nice to Diana like I was being. I think that's why Moose was with us. So we got in there, and Johnny gave me a little saw, like you know, like a rechargeable thing. A Dremel, I think it's called? And then Johnny said we had to cut off Diana's little finger. And he said I had to do it. Well, Diana began to scream under the bag, just scream and scream and Johnny said:

Johnny: You forgot you who you are, my Giant. You a soldier in a war now. You gonna hurt her and get money and dat's who you are. You owe me this, my Giant. I got you a home and a coat, I got you a way to live and a man to be. Dat means I'm your fadder now, and as your fadder I command you to cut off her little finga.

Brian turns to the audience.

Brian: Everything mighta gone differently, if Johnny hadn't said that last part. Johnny was a lot of things, but he was *not* my father. My father was good and he was strong, and he was smart, and raised me right. So, I said:

Brian returns to the warehouse.

Get the fuck off me, man! Blood's gonna spurt from this bitch and I don't wanna get it on my coat.

And Johnny smiled and relaxed a little. And Moose heard what I said about spurting, and he was wearing his rare O.J. Simpson football jersey, so he leaned back a bit too.

I turned on the saw and got ready to cut off Diana's finger, but then at the last second . . .

Brian flies into action

I cut off Moose's finger instead, a coupla his fingers, I think! And Johnny was pulling out his gun, so I had to take care of him fast! I used the only fight move I had. I grabbed him by his neck and rammed him up against a wall.

Brian slams Johnny up against the wall.

When his head hit the wall, it was pretty hard. There was blood there and Johnny seemed knocked out.

Diana pulled the bag off of her head and grabbed up the saw. She used it like a club, but it was still running. She hit Moose with the saw around his head and neck, screaming the whole time. Blood was flying everywhere and Moose looked pretty much dead.

He looks over at Moose.

Yeah. Moose was dead. Yeah. He was dead.

I gently took the saw from her. She stood there looking around and breathing in loud high gulps.

Diana: Where's Johnny?

Brian: OH!

Brian runs to where he left Johnny, and finds nothing.

But Johnny was gone.

The performer transforms to Patrick.

Patrick: I do not know if you have ever been involved in a high-profile kidnapping case, but it is an extraordinary experience, let me tell you. Police swarmed in and set up tables of technology. So many dedicated professionals stand ready for the situation, it's a wonder that criminals have any chance at all.

Seeing the proficiency of law enforcement, it reminded me of the veracity of one of my rules of living, which is sold in booklet and poster forms all over the world as well as of course in the lobby. It is: Do Not Break the Law. For when one lives as we do, the law can seem silly, and perhaps it is. But remember that you might face a judge. And when one faces a judge, your noble philosophy will be arrayed against you, and as with the early Christians, some will suggest that simply believing as you do, you deserve *extra* punishment. I was persecuted for my beliefs during my divorce and it is indeed horrible.

So I co-operated utterly, even as I stayed cocooned in my philosophy. When worry would get the better of me, I would use the Ten Selfish Thoughts technique and the —

He utters three short, quick breaths.

— Breaths of Me-ness.

At this point, I was still me, but that was all to change. Because in the morning I received an envelope from FedEx. Inside was a severed finger, and the nail polish matched my daughter's.

We return to the warehouse, moments after we left.

Diana: Where's Johnny?

Brian: Johnny's gone. He musta left, he musta slipped out when I came to check on you and you were killin' Moose. Oh shit. You killed Moose.

Diana: Yeah, I — Uh —

Diana collapses crying.

Brian: And I knew I hadta take charge of stuff. So I said:

We gotta go.

And she kind of nodded. I peeked outside to see if Johnny's Hummer was there. It wasn't. We took the keys and phone and gun off of Moose and got into his car. Even with the seats pushed way back I looked like a guy in a clown car.

"We go to the police!" I said. I thought this was a good solution to immediate problems, as well as a nice, unselfish thing for me to do, being the criminal in the car. But she said no. She wanted to go to this apartment she had. She said it was a secret apartment she hid from her Dad. It was in her roommate's name but her roommate was in Thailand. And I saw she had something in her hands, and then I could see . . . it was one of Moose's fingers.

Diana: I guess I wanted to see just how far it would go. Just how much was this not his fault? How much did he not care anyway?

We join Detective Stone and Patrick at the mansion.

Detective Stone: When the FedEx guy shows up I think: Here we go. He signs for it and the evidence guys got it and we try to shield the vic usually, but not this time. And there we have the finger. And I can see right then and there that something is off. As the kidnapper police, I see more than my fair share of severed fingers. And unless his daughter is three hundred pounds, Hispanic, and *male*, there is no fucking way this is her finger. But I don't say shit. I wanna see what this does to the guy.

He excuses himself, just like polite, you know? And he leaves the room.

The performer transforms to Patrick.

Patrick: That day, I learned something about myself. I have a *limit*. Everyone has one, and most people never come within miles of it. But then I saw the severed finger of my daughter. And I reached my absolute breaking point. My *limit*.

I was in a haze. I can admit this now. I was so far in, you see. I had said those terrible things to the kidnappers and they cut off a part of my daughter. This was my fault. I knew it. It — it — it was my fault and it was my problem. And I started my usual mantra, "I am all that matters, I am all that matters," but scenes of horror crept in. Her finger, her tiny finger. What sort of implement did they use to take it off? How clean was it? Is an infection building even as we speak?

Was she already dead?

I went downstairs and climbed under my pool table. It's ironic now, isn't it? The combination was her birthday.

The performer transforms to Detective Stone.

Detective Stone: And it finally worked. He comes upstairs with this black duffel bag and he piles the money at my feet. The guy looked just wrecked. He says:

Patrick: Is it enough? It's more than they asked for, but is it enough?

The performer transforms to Brian.

Brian: We got to Diana's place and it was nice. I tried to take the finger from her, you know. I was worried she was crazy, maybe having saw trauma, but she seemed like she had a plan. I saw her painting the nail pink like her nails. I asked her what she was doing and she said:

Diana: I'm teaching my father a lesson.

Brian shrugs, and then starts to feel sick.

Brian: After a while I started to get the shakes and sweats. She didn't have any heroin, but she had some Valium, so I took that. It was the first time I had gone without for weeks and weeks. I wanted some for sure, but where could I score that Johnny wouldn't hear about it? And what if I got high and then Johnny showed up? I'd be useless to Diana, and that scared me more than anything.

It sounds crazy, but this is how I got clean.

I stayed at Diana's place and she took care of me the whole time. I screamed and swore and I threw up a lot and sweated even more, but she was always there with a cool cloth and a fresh bucket.

After two days my head felt clear for the first time in years. I started to really think, you know? And what I thought was that I was pretty fucked. I couldn't figure any way that Johnny wouldn't wanna kill me. I had to get rid of him somehow. But how?

The performer transforms to Patrick.

Patrick: So there I was. A wreck of a man. Are you surprised at me? Do you wonder that I changed so utterly, seeing a flash of gore. I was praying that there would be another phone call, another chance. And then the phone rang.

We hear a phone ring. Brian is making a call.

Brian: Johnny was pretty surprised when I called him. He was like –

Johnny: What de fuck?

Brian: But when I told him, "I'm scared!" he believed me. He had seen me scared a lot, almost our whole relationship, really. I said, "If you meet me at the warehouse, I'll give back Diana and everything can go back like it was!" He was pretty into that. I knew when I got there he'd kill me if he could. So I had to get there first. And I had to take . . . *precautions.*

The performer transforms to Diana, back at the addiction group.

Diana: So public opinion is pretty split on what I did, right? Like some people think my Dad had it coming, and some people think that I'm a terrible bitch to put him through it. It's controversial, which is I guess why I got so much money for my life story. Maybe the last part was maybe a little much.

The performer transforms to Brian.

Brian: Chinatown felt real strange to be in. People stared even more than usual. When I went into Wing's shop, he looked real scared. I wonder who was more scared, you know? I bet me. I had my hat down low and I could feel the little Darth Vader thing taped to my throat. I told him:

Voice switch to Darth Brian.

I am a demon who was enslaved by an evil man. Will you help me, and free us both? And he said:

The performer transforms to Wing. Wing nods. We hear a phone ring.

Patrick: Hello?

Diana: Daddy?

Patrick: Diana, thank God! Tell the man I'll do what he says. I — I — I have the money. I have more than he wanted. Your finger. I'm so sorry about your finger, my daughter. I am so sorry.

Diana: They say it's too late, Daddy. They say they're going to kill me.

Patrick: What? NO! No, I have the money here. Right here. I have the car as well, a Lincoln Navigator, he said. Tell him I have it.

Diana: It's too late, Daddy. They don't care about the money anymore. They say it's the principle, Daddy. It's the principle of the thing.

Patrick: No, I have the money, I have it right here. I can get more as well, if they want. Anything. Anything —

Diana: They say they want you to listen, Daddy.

She holds a gun near the phone and fires once. The performer switches to Patrick hearing it.

Patrick: And my daughter was dead.

The warehouse. Johnny enters.

Johnny: You a big disappointment to me, Giant Man. You let me down. Where da fuck did you get a conscience? You be too poor for a conscience! All of this life is just a war between the rich and the poor. You make war on the rich until you're one of dem, den you turn around and make war on the poor fucks like you used to be. You don't know that, then you just waiting in line to get fucked.

Brian: She's just behind that door.

And he went to go see, right? But it wasn't Diana behind the door. It was Wing and all the Chinatown shopkeepers that Johnny had been leaning on and stealing from. And their sons. And their cousins. They had guns and clubs and stuff. Wing kind of nodded to me . . .

The performer transforms to Wing. Wing nods. Brian steps forth.

Brian: . . . and I left. That was the deal. He gets Johnny and I go free for pretending to be a demon. It's a fair deal.

The performer transforms to Patrick.

Patrick: The police left. I was left alone. Left alone with my culpability. For the first time in a decade, I went to the first bar I could find, and I ordered a drink.

The performer transforms to Detective Stone.

Detective Stone: Jeez, I felt bad for the guy. He cared about his daughter. I think he went a little crazy is all.

But also, it's fishy. It wasn't her finger, right? So whose fucking finger was it? As kidnapper police, you spend all your time getting jerked around by the kidnappers. With the girl "dead" I took a coupla sick days, and did some investigating. It took five minutes to find out the daughter was buying coke from this kid Li'l Charles, real name Charles Pisano. Probably fucking him too. He's a streeter for Johnny Curtina, a fairly nefarious motherfucker I hear about from my buddies in vice. So where's Johnny? It turns out Johnny "Three Fingers" Curtina is in a warehouse, all hacked to shit. CSI is looking it over right now. So, okay.

So what about known associates? So, I hear from a buddy that Leo "The Moose" Mendoza is a known associate, and he's down in the morgue, found three days ago in, wait for it, the same fucking warehouse. And get this! He's missing fingers off his hand. I confirm, is he missin' a pinkie? He is. By the way, the morgue boys say the corpse weighs in at about three hundred pounds, and he ain't a Mendoza by marriage. Do I know my fucking severed pinkies or what?

So I ask around about the rest of his crew. Word was he was rolling with this impossibly big white guy. Okay. I leave that there a second.

And, I look into the girl, this supposedly dead daughter, and she has an extra apartment in her friend's name. It's not her place, but she gets a magazine sent there, *Erotica Weekly*. Bah. So I stake it out. Half a day goes by, and out comes an impossibly big white guy. I picked him up, and I sweated him for a while in interrogation.

Poor mutherfucker, you know? He weren't no real crook. He told me everything.

The performer transforms to Brian, sitting in the small chair, in the interrogation room.

Brian: I think that's everything. That's exactly what happened and I didn't even gloss it over to make me look better or anything. So what happens now?

The performer transforms to Detective Stone and regards him coolly a moment.

Detective Stone: You get the fuck outta here. And you leave town.

Brian: Thank you!

Detective Stone turns to the audience.

Detective Stone: Yeah, I let him go.

Fuck it, the guy's a hero, far as I'm concerned. He did my job for me, better than I usually get it done. And Johnny and Moose. Good fuckin' riddance. And I guess the girl is due some punishing, like, legally, but with what she went through? Maybe she's punished enough.

And maybe I'm due some punishing too. But fuck it! I'm retired. Out of country. And I suppose somebody could come out here to fucking Costa Rica and get me for my disciplinary hearing, but I really doubt they will. Cop pension goes pretty far out here, but you can always use some extra, right? That's why I sold my story to you people. Ha. *People* magazine. Used to be I'd sort through death and misery, every day, for a plumber's salary. Now I fish, and the girls come out for Christmases. If you think I got something to be guilty about, well, all due respect, fuck you.

And I kept reading those books by Mr. Spencer. And whatever else Mr. Spencer was, you know, he talked his talk and then he walked his walk. I mean, you gotta respect that a little, right?

You know, I saw so much shit on the force, and a lot of it, I really carried it with me, but I understand now, a lot of that stuff, just wasn't my fault. And if I were to be a thousand percent honest with you, I gotta admit, I don't fucking care anyway.

The performer transforms to Diana.

Diana: So I got my revenge, I guess, but I knew I might never see my Dad again, and I miss him. Is that weird? Revenge is weird, right? It never feels as good as you think it will.

When he said he had the ransom, when I heard him crying, I almost forgot the whole plan. I mean, he cared, for a minute there, and if I had been thinking clearly, I would have been happy to leave it at that. But I was mad. If I could go back in time I would do it all differently, which I guess means I'm growing up?

After the thing with the phone and the gun, I figured Dad might drink. I watched him leave, let myself in with the key and went straight to the floor safe. The combo was my birthday, which I guess is ironic, now. I had been helping myself to a bundle here and a bundle there for years, and now I took the rest. I gave Brian a cool million in an account in his name, and a hundred grand cash.

I mean, sure, a deal's a deal, but he didn't do it for the money. He did because he cared about me. He cared about me when he wasn't supposed to, and my Dad was supposed to care about me and didn't. At least not enough. So Brian got rewarded and Dad got punished. That's fair, right?

The performer transforms to Patrick.

Patrick: And so I was tested. I was sorely tested, and I found my resolve all too weak, but in the end, I was right. I abandoned briefly all my principles and returned to the sentimental life, and what did it get me?

Scorn. Deception. Theft.

I did not seek redress for my stolen money. It's a hurt that feeds me and releases me. That is the last she will ever steal from me. She will get no more of my time, no more of my attention, and no more of my money. I think of it as payment for my certainty. For I stand before you now, newly baptized in my faith, a pure vessel of my philosophy.

Now, more than ever, it is not my fault, and I don't care anyway.

Patrick's last line echoes in the mic. The performer transforms to Brian, sitting in the small chair. He types into a laptop in a café.

Brian: Dear Diana. Amsterdam is nice. The people are taller, most of them, and if I slouch a lot, I can almost fit in. I look forward to your visit. For the first time in a long time, I look forward. Your friend, Brian.

Hopeful music plays as Brian looks out at the passing people. Blackout.

THE END

PORN STAR

PRODUCTION HISTORY

Porn Star had its world premiere in January 2001 as the inaugural production of the new Azimuth Theatre space in Edmonton, Alberta, which wasn't quite done yet.

Starring: Andrea House (pictured on overleaf)
Also Appearing: Chris Craddock, Darrin Hagen, Kevin Gillese
Lighting Design: Chris Craddock
Sound Design: Darrin Hagen
Slide Projection Design: Tandie McLeod
Assistant Director: Kevin Gillese

Porn Star has since been performed by several women across Canada, to whom I am very grateful. They are Jocelyn Ahlf, Cheryl Jack, Shannon Elizabeth, Amanda Bergen, Anne Wyman, Amy Lee, Heather Marie Annis, Sarah Mennel, and Lynne Griffin.

CAST OF CHARACTERS

Esther Kirkenchuck — a librarian
Kate Kirkenchuck — her sister
Sharon Kirkenchuck — her mother
Clarice Dubois — advice columnist
Clarice's boyfriend — a journalist
Voice — the pornographer
Jesus — Jesus
Sarah Palin — aspiring president/figment of Sharon's imagination

PRODUCTION NOTES

Porn Star is the solo show that isn't often a solo show. Certainly it can be made for one lady to take on the entire situation, but often a man has been used as well. My production used three. The latest production (as of this writing) used four women, one for each major character, and it worked a treat. Other productions have included recorded voices, and slides and video and what-have-you. All this is to say there are many ways to skin this cat, so please feel free to find your own.

Esther enters, with her digital recorder. She is doing a vocal warm-up.

Esther: Brrrm, brrrrm. President Sarah Palin. President Sarah Palin. President Sarah Palin. President Sarah Palin. President Sarah Palin. President Sarah Palin. Mmmmah, mmmmmah.

She hits record.

Esther Kirkenchuck. Librarian. Elbow, Saskatchewan. Winner of the Pronto Video Best New Performer July 4, 2012, 11:48 P.M. My life. Hmmm . . .

Her phone rings.

Hello? You keep calling. *Hello?*

Esther returns to her recorder.

So . . . I was having a pretty boring time of it, really. Pretty dull. What was it Grandpa used to say, living life like a leaf, waiting to turn brown. Of course, he was a racist.

I was twenty-eight when it all started to happen. Twenty-eight, and tired of Pilsner boys and their tailgate parties. Tired of never having to look before crossing the street. I was tired of being bored, but too scared to change my life.

But then one day I got this email. And I know all about fake emails since I tried to help that African prince get his money out of Alderaan, but this one caught my eye. The email called me Esther Star, and my name is Esther Kirkenchuck, like I said before. The email said: Congratulations Esther Star, you have been nominated by Pronto Video Productions for the Best New Performer award in our amateur category and do I want to go to San Francisco to attend the ceremony?

What? There must be some mistake. I never heard of Pronto Video. And it sounded like some kind of *pornography company* and I never in my life had anything to do with pornography . . . except . . . Okay, this is embarrassing . . . there was this guy . . . with this one guy I dated who liked to watch it with me . . .

The sound of sex comes up as Esther pictures it.

You know, like before, and sort of . . . during, but I never . . .

We hear a recorded male voice.

Voice: You're a star, baby. You're my Esther Star.

Esther: Except he did call me that. And there were a lot of mirrors at his place, like a weird amount of mirrors. And we always did it with the lights on when we were there. Not just lights, but really bright lights. Like as bright as those up there, you know, like pro-lights, which I thought was weird, but — but that was years ago, and I never watched any pornographies since, even though I didn't always mind watching them, you know, before and . . . during, mmmmm, and then I saw there was a link to the video that was nominated for the award. And I thought, well, let's see what top-quality pornography looks like, you know, to improve my critical depth. The website was very flashy and well-made. The video loaded up and I saw —

Lights change, and Esther is in her porno, being taken roughly from behind. We hear the man speaking heatedly in the background.

OH! OH YEAH!

Voice: Uh! You're a star, baby!

Esther: — yeah, OH GOD!

Voice: What do you do?

Esther: I'm a librarian!

Voice: Yeah?

Esther: FUCK YEAH! I'm a dirty LIBRARIAN!

Lights back to Esther's place.

That . . . I . . . was Esther Star. And I just about died. In fact, I did die and I was in a room with monkeys and banjos but then I came back and there I still was on there on the internet and —

Lights change, and Esther is in her porno. We hear the man speaking heatedly in the background.

Uh, oh God, Oooooh God, OH GOD OOOOH GOOOODDDD!

Lights back to Esther's place.

And I'm not even religious. Anymore. I mean I believe in God and all that, but —

Lights change, and Esther is in her porno.

OH GOD!

Lights go back to Esther's place.

But then almost in spite of myself, I was a little turned on. Because I remembered this guy. I mean, how could I forget? Before him I had sex fourteen times, twelve of those with my old boyfriend who couldn't find my clitoris.

Lights change, and Esther is in her porno.

OH GOD! MY GO-O-OD! OH GOD!

Esther's place.

And he filmed me. I supposed he taped me, or like, hard-drived me, he hard-drived me and he put it on the internet, and men watched it, maybe with their girlfriends before they, and during . . . and . . . .

She gets turned on in spite of herself, and then remembers her anger.

How dare that bastard tape me like that and put it on the internet . . . where men would watch it, while they . . . or maybe with their girlfriends . . . before and, like, during . . . and –

Lights change, and Esther is in her porno.

OH GOD!

Esther's place.

Oh, I have to see that again –

She rewinds. Lights change, and Esther is in her porno.

OH GOD!

Esther's place.

You know, I really like my hair back then. It was just the right length and that colour is just right and –

Lights change, and Esther is in her porno.

OH GOD!

Esther's place.

– and I wonder if he's gonna be there. Pronto Video doesn't know who I am. He's going to the ceremony I bet. He wants to see me in San Francisco. At the awards. Hm. I was nominated for an award. An award for my –

Lights change, and Esther is in her porno.

OH GOD!

Esther's place.

Well, that's nice, isn't it? To be appreciated. To be recognized. And he's almost definitely gonna be there. I could give him a piece of my mind . . . and maybe . . . a piece . . . of my . . .

Her phone rings.

Hello? Hello? Who is this?

We join Kate in Hell.

Kate: A lot people think that if you commit suicide you go to Hell. And they're right. I killed myself at fourteen and that's exactly what happens. It goes like this. You slip into unconsciousness, and you wake up in a room where a thousand monkeys are playing detuned banjos with violin bows. You start to walk but then you fall down a pit and you fall and fall and your flesh is stripped from your bones and your skeleton keeps falling and then your bones land all in a chalky white pile. Then you are painfully reborn and you instantly grow to full size, pausing only to re-experience puberty. Then, just as you're getting your period — BANG you're in the room with the monkeys and the banjos and it happens all over again. That's what hell is like. It sucks donkey-cock.

But you get a break, if you want — and who wouldn't? You get to take a break and visit your own funeral. My mother was there looking so sad that I almost felt sorry I did it. But more, she looked guilty. She looked like she knew it was all her fault, like she would never be whole again. I was so happy I almost did a little dance except I didn't have a body to do it in. Not even a ghostly one like in the movies.

My mother looked so sad that I couldn't help but feel like *the bitch was finally getting what she deserved* and I could really get on with my life and be happy. Then I remembered how I was dead and in hell and had fucked it all up.

When you're fourteen and you kill yourself, you always sort of think you can take it back and live some more, maybe thinner and with better clothes, but that's not how it goes. Instead it's monkeys and banjos and being on the rag. I'll never kill myself at fourteen again.

The podcast studio. Clarice speaks into a microphone.

Clarice: It says on my business card that I'm Clarice DuBois, syndicated advice columnist and podcast darling. But people rarely write me for advice. They write to me for a permission slip. I want my boyfriend to pee on me. Am I a freak? I love to sniff ladies' sneakers. Are there any more out there like me? I'm gonna say this once because I'm tired of writing it down. There are always more like you. Whatever freaky, dirty little thing you can dream up, there's an entire community of people out there doing it. Lemme tell you. Into fellating shaved goats while listening to George Michael on a runaway tractor? Have I got a website for you! Trust me. You're not that creative. Sex has been around for a long time, and people have been energetically experimenting since its inception. Whatever you got going on, others had goin' on in ancient Egypt and rural Ukraine and Manhattan in the eighties. There's nothing new under the sun. So when people write to me and say, "Am I weird?" I say, "Yes, you are." They ask, "Is it okay that I do this?" And all I can say is . . . "It's okay with me."

Boyfriend: Clarice. Are you almost done? We're late.

Clarice: You sit right there, handsome. I just have one more of these to do. Don't make that face. I'll be right there.

She turns to her microphone.

And now my first letter. Dear Clarice, I'm plagued by a controlling man. He makes my life hell.

She glances back at her boyfriend before continuing.

A church/TV studio. We hear angry organ. Sharon Kirkenchuck preaches to her flock. She unrolls a piece of Scotch Tape.

Sharon: Sex is like tape. Tape is so sticky the first time it's applied. Sex is like that. Sex is so sticky with our hearts and minds the first time we use it.

She puts the tape on her arm, then rips it off.

Ouch! But try applying that tape a second time.

She does.

It doesn't stick as well then, does it? And a third time, even less sticky. And a fourth time, and we're lucky if the tape has any glue to it at all.

Sex is like that. Sex is exactly like this tape.

When you use sex for recreation, you're wasting the stickiness of your tape. And when it comes time for marriage, and you want the tape to attach you forever, body and soul, to the special love you've chosen, you'd best have sticky, sticky tape. And not tape that's been stuck and unstuck to every Tom Dick and Harry that came along. Now life is short and pleasure can be hard to find in a cruel, godless world like ours, and shouldn't we try to get all we can? You're half right. Life is short. So very, very, short. And do you know what's long?

Eternity.

Eternity is very, very long! So think of eternity when you think of grabbing the gusto! Think of the baby Jesus crying when you sin! Think of that man and what he really wants from you! Think of your tape, and how sticky you'll want it to be when the time comes! Sticky enough to keep you stuck to your man! Sticky enough to keep you stuck in your family! Sticky enough to keep you stuck in your life, until the little baby Jesus calls you home!

She sings.

Fairest Lord Jesus . . .

Esther's place. She has been recording the TV.

Esther: Did you hear that? That's my Mom. That's her on her old TV show. My Dad was a big preacher in the States before he got caught with those boy-hookers. My Mom could have been destroyed by it, but instead she took over his church. She's really strong, I guess. She got a talk radio show and some people call her Rush Limbaugh with a vagina. Americans love her because she had the integrity to move away from a perfectly good public health care system. My Mom is also president of the Sarah Palin for President committee, which is I think officially the last committee that thinks Sarah Palin should be President. Mom tells me about it when she calls me on the phone.

Sharon: Esther? It's your mother.

Esther: Hi, Mom. How's it going?

Sharon: Exciting. In a word, it is going in a very exciting way for all of us here in America. The winds of change are blowing, dear Esther, and instead of a dirty wind of loosening morals and inattention to the scriptures, it is a clean wind of beauty and truth. Sarah Palin is so dynamic, so fresh, like Reagan, but *alive*, like Kennedy, but *female*. We'll show them what God's people can do! Now we need the White House, and only Sarah can win it.

Esther: You really think so?

Sharon: Can I be honest with you, Esther?

Esther: Yes.

Sharon: I was visited.

Esther: By Sarah Palin?

Sharon: By Jesus. I was visited in a dream by Jesus Christ Himself and He told me that it was my path to help make Sarah Palin the president of these United States of America.

Esther: I didn't know she was running.

Sharon: Right now, she's not, but if I could just talk to her, woman to woman, share my holy vision, I know I could change her mind. I have not felt this kind of purpose since I was called to preach! Finally I'm involved in something that means something.

Esther: I was gonna mention motherhood at this point, but I couldn't fit it in.

Sharon: President Sarah Palin. Isn't it a beautiful grouping of words? President Sarah Palin.

Esther: Try saying that ten times fast. It's like a tongue twister. President Sarah Palin President Sarah Palin. It's hard to say fast! Try it. President Sarah Palin President Sarah Palin President Sarah Palin! . . . You're not doing it.

Small pause. Sharon makes a face.

Sharon: I have to go, Esther.

Esther: Um, Kate's birthday is coming up, you know, and I was thinking we could get together and put some flowers out at the cemetery and maybe get a coffee or something.

Sharon: Well, I would, um, Kate is uh, I would love to, but I am so busy right now, what with uh, Sarah Palin. Why don't you take a picture of the flowers and email it to me at my office and then, when I get a free moment, I can . . . you know . . . uh, mourn.

Esther: Okay.

Sharon: Okay. Goodbye, Esther. Be good.

She hangs up.

Esther: When we were kids, me and Kate used to play escape. She was amazing. I would tie her up and put her in the dryer and block the door and start it up, and by the time I got upstairs to make toast, she was there with orange juice.

Sharon: I love you, Esther. Be good.

Esther: I'm going to San Francisco.

We join Kate in Hell.

Kate: I was alive once. I walked to school and ate my lunch and had a boyfriend. That was the problem. I had a boyfriend. I was too young to date. That's what Mother said. I was too young and boys only want one thing . He wasn't like us anyway. He wasn't a Christian. Well, he was Anglican, but it's not the same.

We walked down by the creek. I told him about my nightmares and he told me about his parents. He took my hand and it felt like electricity. We lay on our backs while the water trickled past our sneakers and the clouds transformed. I told him about my mother and he told me about his nightmares. He turned his head and I turned mine. Our breath mingled, minty from gum, and when he kissed me it was like I turned to light. We didn't know anything, so we did everything.

Afterwards I lay there breathing, and breathing. It was suddenly amazing that air came in and out of me. And below my lungs, in my belly, I felt a special heat. An almost throbbing, living difference in me. I figured that this new heat was me, having become a woman, instead of a little girl. I figured that other women would recognize the change and treat me with a new respect. But I was wrong. It doesn't show. Not for months.

We join Clarice in the podcast studio.

Clarice: There's been a lot of talk about Tantric sex. You never come in Tantric sex, you redirect all your energies away from your genitals and throughout your body. You hardly ever have an orgasm, but then when you finally do, it goes on for hours and days. People are reporting orgasms that go on for ten hours and I suppose it's wonderful, but I can't help but think — Don't you have a job? Who has time to orgasm for ten hours? Sorry, I can't do lunch Monday, I've got an orgasm from nine right through to six-thirty. Tuesday? No, orgasming. Wednesday is possible, but I might still be orgasming so I better text you. Imagine the scheduling alone! As a busy career woman, I only have regular forty-five minute sex with standard-issue ten-second orgasms, and I can still barely fit it in before the pizza gets here and *The Bachelorette* comes on. I can hardly fit it in some days, and as an expert, I get to write it off on my taxes. Ten-hour orgasms must be a thing for the rich and the unemployed. Statistics say that poor people have more sex and better sex than rich people, and I guess that's why there's so many more of them. It's possible I'm oversimplifying. I'm Clarice DuBois, saying if you can't get laid, go fuck yourself.

Boyfriend: Clarice, are you done now? We're really late.

Clarice: Yes, darling. I am all done and now you can have all of me to yourself. Aren't you the lucky one? Don't make that face. I'm coming right now. You go bring the car around. Go ahead. Go on, handsome.

He begins to walk away.

I love to watch you walk away. You are a beautiful man. Mm! You're gorgeous!

Her boyfriend walks out.

Jesus suffering fuck. Men are such hard work.

We join Esther at her place.

Esther: Clarice DuBois! Isn't she great? If I wrote a letter to her right now it would say, "Dear Clarice, should I go to San Francisco to see this guy who taped me having sex and put it on the internet?" And she'd probably say —

Clarice: You should be calling a lawyer, not planning a visit.

Esther: But . . . I haven't been nominated for an award for a long time. Not since the English award in Grade Twelve, which I won, thank you very much. I won for my short story about the bears. But I think I was the sympathy vote. Because of my sister Kate, and her dying like she did. I remember my mother sitting in the audience, looking up, proud. Mom. Proud ashamed proud ashamed proud ashamed. Of me. Of me and Kate . . . Kate.

We join Kate in Hell.

Kate: When I think of it, it was probably more of a "cry for help" thing than a "me really trying to die" thing. I couldn't think of anything to make it even remotely okay with Mom. And I couldn't tell him, because Mom said that you can't tell boys you're pregnant, because then they move to other towns and change their names. And in an alternate reality, I take care of that baby. And it beams love at me through its tiny face forever and I wear aprons and have wisdom. But in this reality, I open Mom's medicine cabinet. I hide in the treehouse and I take one of Mom's Valium. And then I take another one and then another one and then another one and then another one and then another one and then another one and then another one and then . . .

Clarice breezes in.

Clarice: Darling, darling. I'm so sorry I'm late.

Boyfriend: You're always late.

Clarice: But I'm always worth it. This is strange, no? You interviewing me? Intimate, yet impersonal.

Boyfriend: I'm a journalist, Clarice.

Clarice: I thought you were a blogger.

Boyfriend: Bloggers can be journalists.

Clarice: Yes they can. And I want you to know that I take you very seriously.

Boyfriend: I'm turning on the recorder. Clarice DuBois, take one. Here we go. Clarice, you have never denied the rumours of your bisexuality.

Clarice: Well, I'll deny them now. I'm omnisexual, as you well know. I've enjoyed sex with men and women and some animals and the odd vegetable in this long life of mine.

I've been with rubber implements, some that wiggle and others that you fill up with hot water. I've had sex in tents, houses, and cars, trains, planes and camelback, all alone and in crowds. My authority is based on experience.

Boyfriend: Your advice column has recently been boycotted by the Christian Defence League. Any reaction?

Clarice: I have only pity for those who let an invisible man in the sky keep them from a good boink when obviously they desperately need one.

Boyfriend: I understand you've received threats.

Clarice: I get a lot of kooky letters. Some threaten to kill me, others want me to mail them my panties. I don't fear for my life until it's absolutely necessary, and I don't post underwear. That's my policy and it's served me well.

Boyfriend: So you don't take their threats seriously.

Clarice: There's far too many abortion doctors running free to worry some Christian extremist is gonna cap me. There's a lot of gay politicians to murder yet, and don't forget this hip new pope. I'm strictly small potatoes.

Boyfriend: You really want to say that about the pope?

Clarice: I'm being shocking. Journalists like that.

Boyfriend: I'm a journalist. I know what journalists like.

Clarice: Yes! I take you very seriously.

Small pause.

Boyfriend: I have inside informants who state that you belittle your boyfriend constantly. That you treat him as a lesser creature because he isn't famous.

Clarice: What?

Boyfriend: That you keep younger men so that sex is constantly available to you but that you don't care about them. That you keep them waiting. Sometimes for hours.

Clarice: Who are your informants? *You're* my boyfriend.

Boyfriend: Am I? Because I feel like more of a servant.

Pause.

Clarice: Is the tape recorder turned off? . . . Turn the tape recorder off.

Ex-Boyfriend: It's off.

Clarice: So. What's happened?

Ex-Boyfriend: You treat me badly. Anyway, I met someone.

Clarice: Someone? Who someone?

Ex-Boyfriend: Someone . . . quiet.

Clarice: Quiet? I'm QUIET!

She speaks more quietly.

How do you mean, quiet?

Ex-Boyfriend: Somebody who enjoys sex, but doesn't need an international column advocating it.

Clarice: Oh, I see. Right. The strain getting to you, hm? Can't cope with a lady more famous than you?

Ex-Boyfriend: That's not it.

Clarice: You fucking caveman! Of course that's it. Get out. Just get out. This interview is cancelled. I ungive my permission!

Ex-Boyfriend: Clarice –

Clarice: Get the fuck OUT!

He does.

Jesus Christ. Men are so fucking stupid.

We join Kate in Hell.

Kate: Here's something you might not know. Occasionally, in Hell, the Devil throws a party for all the suicides who killed themselves because of God. Most of the guests are gay teenagers. Satan thinks it's hilarious. Satan laughs and laughs. He has an infectious laugh. Not the kind of infectious that makes you want to laugh too, but the kind that gives you the flu. Don't get too close to Satan when he's laughing. If you think Hell is bad, you should try Hell with the flu. This is bad news for me, 'cause Satan always wants to hang out with me, on account of my mother being a preacher. He sits with me and pats my bum and it's totally sexual harassment, but what am I gonna do? And as if it wasn't uncomfortable enough, he's always changing shape. First he's a giant squid with tentacles that all have Hitler's head on the end. Then he's Sammy Davis Jr. and Al Jolson, sharing a body. Then he's a giant ape with a talking penis that snakes down to laugh in your face and before you know it, you've got the flu. So I'm at one of these parties, sitting with the Devil, who at the moment is a giant pierced udder that leaks sour milk and suddenly it occurs to me . . . I've gotta get out of here.

We join Clarice in the podcast studio.

Clarice: Believe it or don't, sports fans, but it seems I am single. Again. Once more a straight man has found the nerve to dump a bona fide sex expert, discouraging amateurs everywhere. Without generalizing, I would say the problem is that *men are all the same*. Oh, they like a brassy broad for a little while. But when it comes time for the long haul, what they really want is a supportive little housekeeper, who shuts the hell up at parties. Men can't date anyone smarter, louder, or funnier than they are, and with all due respect to my ex, which is very little, I was all three, and better in bed to boot! Men can be terrified, skittish creatures, and they shrink up if they try to punch above their weight and fail. I was complaining in this way to my best gay, and he suggested I was simply dating the wrong kind of men, and I must agree. So for the time being, I will date the right kind of men. What kind is that, you ask?

Women.

We hear the sound of the plane taking off. Esther sits excitedly in her seat.

Esther: On the plane they had satellite, but I just looked out the window. I saw a woman go into the lavatory and a man follow just a little too quickly behind her. You know, when you stop to look around yourself, it's like, sex is everywhere. Everywhere I am, anyway. I try to sleep and all I can see is him.

We hear the male voice from earlier.

Voice: You're a star baby.

Esther: His eyes and mouth and hands and eyes and legs and eyes and lips and tongue and chest and his eyes. Did I mention his eyes?

Voice: You are so beautiful.

Esther: We met at a bar in town. I was drinking with the elementary teacher set. A lotta cardigans. He wore a tight black T-shirt.

Voice: You aren't driving home, are you?

Esther: We went for late-night breakfast at Humpty's. We talked but we didn't say anything. Just jokes and gibberish and made-up words.

Voice: Flarn. Tpottle.

Esther: No, you are.

Voice: No, you are.

Esther: No, you are.

Voice: No, you are.

Esther: No, you are.

Voice: No, you.

Esther: He put his hand up to my mouth and I bit his fingers.

Voice: You gonna finish that?

Esther: I thought of my mother and it just made me want to more. Just that feeling. That feeling of being bad. It feels so good. It's just crazy.

Voice: Nice place you've got here.

Esther: He pulled me close and undid my bra with one hand. I was so impressed. My Mom shouldn't've been warning me about high school guys. It was guys like these that were the problem.

Voice: You are so beautiful.

Esther: And I was. I was so beautiful. I was hot. I was so —

Her cell phone rings.

My cell phone. I turned off my cell phone. This is impossib –

She answers.

Hello? MY CELL PHONE IS TURNED OFF, WHO THE HELL ARE YOU? – I'm sorry. It's just the phone – but I did turn it off, that's WHY I'M – No, no no, there's no need to land the plane. I am so sorry. Sorry. Yes. Shhh. I will. Sorry.

We join Kate in Hell.

Kate: So I'm in the room with the monkeys and the banjoes, trying to figure my escape. I find this extra banjo and bow and I play that for a while. The monkeys don't seem to notice. And after a while a bell rings and all the monkeys start filing out. They all go through a door and down a hall. At the end of the hall is a swimming pool. One by one the monkeys jump in and dissolve. Soon the swimming pool is brown with monkey. Then some zombies come in, damned like me, I guess. They start to spoon water out of the pool and into little jars labeled monkey. When the pool is drained, and it takes a while, believe me, they all file out and I follow them. They put the jars of monkey on a shelf and go down a hall to a bigger pool. Then they jump in and dissolve. Another bunch of people start scooping out that pool. Their eyes are all glassy like zombies, but none of them try to eat my brains. I back off, like, three steps and suddenly I'm on this busy street. There's demons walking around with shopping bags from the Gap and drinking on the patio. There's a lady working in a bake shop that I think might be Marie Antoinette. I think so, because her head floated about two inches above her neck, and she constantly recommended the cake. I'm just staring like a tourist when this streetcar whizzes by. It is full of lawyers clutching briefcases and looking nervous. The sign on it says INCOMING. Another one goes by the opposite way, but it's empty. I figure it's going to pick up new souls, from the entrance, I guess, and an entrance is a door and that's just what I need. I hop onto the empty streetcar and I'm on my way. Streetcars. Huh. Hell reminds me a lot of —

Esther: San Francisco! It's crazy here, you know? There are people on the street twenty-four hours a day. Three PM Sunday, people on the street. Four AM Thursday, people on the street. And even though it's a big city, I feel safer here than I do at home. In Elbow I could get stabbed on Main Street and no one would find me for hours. Not here. Too many people on the street. I take a cab to the hotel. At the hotel, I unwrap all the glasses and set up my mini ironing board and roll on the sheets. Then I go down to the hotel bar for a drink. And I think since this is a big city, maybe a famous person will walk up to me and say hi, but then I think, "Oh that's stupid, famous people don't just say hi to strangers."

Clarice: Hi there.

Esther: And then, one does.

Clarice: You're not from around here, are you?

Esther: What? Me? Born and bred. I'm a Franciscan, a San-Franner, from just down near . . . You can tell, huh?

Clarice: Only by the nice. I'm Clarice DuBois. I'm from everywhere.

Esther: Oh — You're — Oh! You're the sex lady!

Clarice: You've heard of me.

Esther: My mother sure hates you.

Clarice: Oh? Is she a Christian? Frigid? Both?

Esther: She's, uh, a Christian, a big one, in politics and all that, so —

Clarice: What did you say your last name was?

Esther: Kirkenchuck.

Clarice: Jesus Suffering Fuck. Is your mother Sharon Kirkenchuck?

Esther: No.

Clarice: Okay. What brings you here?

Esther: I got nominated for an award. For, uh, performing. The ceremony is tomorrow night, in the big ballroom.

Clarice: The Pronto Video Awards ceremony?

Esther: No.

Clarice: Let's recap. I'm sitting here with Sharon Kirkenchuck's daughter, who is nominated for an award as a performer by Pronto Video?

Esther: It's just an amateur award. I'm an amateur. Amateur performer.

Clarice: Fabulous meeting you.

Esther: And we started talking. It seemed so easy somehow. I didn't worry about anything I told her, because I knew from her column she wasn't the judging kind. And I guess I got really used to talking to the judging type people, because it was so refreshing to just say all the things that I really think. If I said these things to anybody in Elbow, Saskatchewan they would just burst into flames or drown me for a witch or something. But everything's freer in the big city. You can be yourself. Or you can be a new self. I wasn't sure which one I was being. We got drunker and drunker and talked more and more and Clarice asked me up to her room for a hoot. I said we were already having a hoot. A hoot and a holler, like my grandpa used to say. But she said that wasn't what she meant. Upstairs she pulled out a . . . marijuana cigarette, you know, a joint, like, drugs. And I was going to say no, like I always did, on both occasions that I was offered illegal substances. But the new me or the real me, whichever I was being, thought a hoot would be just the thing. I guess that a hoot is like a truth serum, because Clarice and me talked and talked and I told her my whole life and she told me hers and we became best friends and then I woke up in my own hotel room. I woke up happy because of my new best friend.

I started to brush my teeth like it was a normal day, but then I remembered real suddenly that it's not. Today is the day of the awards. I wanna vomit and I wanna eat and I want to die and I have a vague urge to masturbate all mixed up in my head. I dunno if I've ever been so excited. I spend most of the day with cucumber slices over my eyes, drinking mineral water, because that's what the supermodels say: hydrate hydrate hydrate. Which is also a good idea for me on account of being a bit hungover. I'm nervous about the award, because even though I don't have much of a critical depth in amateur porn, I'd sure like to win, because, it's just better than losing. But mostly, I'm nervous about him being there. About seeing him again. Him. I've imagined it a hundred times just today, so about nine million times total. It always sort of goes like this.

Voice: My God, Esther, Can it be you?

Esther: It's me. It's all of me.

Voice: I've prayed to God for this day.

Esther: And then usually we're in the jungle and all he's wearing is this pile of velvet snakes that reach out and pull me close to his muscly chest, and then usually we're on a plane on a jumbo heart-shaped bed and he reaches over and grabs my chin and says —

Voice: Your skin looks great.

Esther: Because I've always been a bit insecure about my skin and I like to hear that it looks good, because I try hard, you know?

Voice: Let me worship you.

Esther: Is what he usually says next and then he does, you know, worship me, and then I worship him for a while and then we fuck. Worship means oral sex. You knew that, right?

Voice: I love you, Esther. I've always loved you and I always will.

Esther: Is what he says last. He always says it. And depending on my mood I say, "I love you too" or "Worship me," or if I'm feeling kind of worldly and bitter I say, "You should know better than to fall in love with a girl like me. I am the wind. I am the lioness. I must be free." But usually I imagine that I love him too and then we get married and then I get to imagine the wedding night, and he is almost always fabulous, because he's really me and I certainly know where my clitoris is. I was just finishing being carried over the threshold when Clarice came to get me.

Clarice: Darling. You look fabulous.

Esther: Really? Do you think I look fabulous?

She faces out.

Suddenly I really care what Clarice thinks about how I look. I care like she was my date or a guy or something.

Clarice: Would I lie to you? Now you lie to me.

Esther: I don't have to. You look really beautiful, Clarice.

She faces out.

And she does! She looks so good I just want to eat her up and the way she looks affects me just like she was a guy or something.

Clarice: Aren't you the sweetest little prairie thing. There must be sincerity in wheat.

Esther turns to the audience.

Esther: And I giggled the way I might giggle if I was nervous about going out, which I was but more I was nervous about going out with Clarice, sort of like if she was, I dunno, a guy or something. I was afraid I might say something dumb, so I just said, "Are you ready to go?" And she was, so off we went. Down the elevator and down the hall and toward the ballroom. I was so nervous that I was getting a bit unsteady on my feet and I grabbed Clarice's hand. We were holding hands when we entered and that's why everything went how it did. If we hadn't been holding hands my Mom would probably still be in politics and she wouldn't be in that home, and maybe I'd still be a librarian. But we were holding hands when we got there and Clarice is so famous, so —

A thousand flashbulbs go off and Esther poses for the pictures.

— and I hardly thought anything of it at the time, just that it was fabulous to be an award-nominated performer. But right at that moment my mother was at a Tea Party fundraiser, saying —

Sharon is at a podium.

Sharon: Too many think only of men when they think of homosexuality! Don't forget the lesbians. Don't forget the sick women and their slavish desires for . . . VAGINA!

We flash back and forth.

Esther: So later when a reporter asked if she was aware her daughter was a lesbian porn star, she could only say —

Sharon: I was not aware of that. I'll haveta look that up.

We rejoin Esther at the awards reception.

Esther: But I didn't know about that yet. I just knew that I had never seen such a party. All those people.

A swirl of characters.

— Well, sure I'll eat his ass. Just no kissing.

— And he's like UH UH UH, and I'm like what?

— I appreciated the watch, but what I really need is a penis enlargement.

— Mommy, can I have a soda?

— And then he's like UUUH UUUH UUUUUH!

— All I'm saying is, if you're going to be doing anal scenes, lay off the Mexican food!

— And then he's like AAAAUH! AAAAAUH! AAAAUH!

— The funny thing about guys who get sex changes is that they immediately start keeping the bathroom cleaner.

— Hey, isn't that John Wayne Bobbitt?

— And then he's like UUUAHRG! AUUAAARGH! UUUAAAARRRGH!

— Two words. Scar. Tissue.

— And then I realize he isn't having an orgasm. He's dying!

— Fuck you, I may be in porn, but I'm also a Catholic.

— And that's how I lost my Uncle Tommy.

— It's too big. If he gets an erection, he passes out from blood loss to his brain.

— I'm in porn right now. But what I'd really like is to be a professional wrestler.

— Sure, he was a dwarf. But you couldn't tell by his cock.

Voice: Esther Kirkenchuck. Is that you?

Esther thrills to the sound of his voice.

Esther: And it was him. I knew that voice. This was the moment. The moment I had imagined. I prepared myself mentally for utter fabulousness and then I turned around —

She turns around.

And there he was, all of him, in the flesh and he was . . . shorter than I remembered. And he had a new moustache that I didn't like at all. And he was . . . way shorter than I remembered. And he had a little belly on him that he might have had before, but I erased in my head when I thought of him. I had erased the rather large earlobes that he had as well, and in my head he was . . . definitely taller. I tried to picture him wearing a pile of velvet snakes and I just –

Voice: What's so funny?

Esther: It's just so funny to see you. After all this time.

Voice: I was afraid you'd be mad at me.

Esther: Well – and then I *was* mad at him. Just then all of a sudden there he was in front of me, short and pudgy and with a moustache, and I was so mad at him for not being more attractive . . . that I decided to get mad at him for taping me having sex. Well, that makes sense, doesn't it?

Voice: You *are* mad at me.

Esther: You're damn right I'm mad. My body is a temple, mister, and before you tape the temple you ask the . . . priestess and then I pass the plate of . . . permission. Well, you didn't ask the priestess and I don't know what kind of money you made on that website, but I'm going to sue you for all of it.

Voice: And you have a great case. But, the website's really taking off, so it would be great if we could make a deal. Here's some contracts for you to consider, and a cheque for your royalties to this point.

Esther: So it's bribery, is it? You think a few grand is a trade for my dignity?

Voice: The cheque is for two hundred and sixty-three thousand dollars.

Esther: Oh. Oh. So, I will have a lawyer look at these.

She takes the papers.

Let's go, Clarice.

Voice: Wait. Can't we talk a bit? I've . . . I've missed you.

Esther: And then I softened just a little bit. He missed me, which was much more like my fantasy than a second ago. And then I saw Clarice there, and it seemed like there was a choice to make, and to be honest, it wasn't any choice at all. I said, "You can talk to my lawyer," and me and Clarice walked away.

Clarice: Who's that?

Esther: He's the guy. The guy who taped me.

Clarice: So I gathered. But what's his name?

Esther: It's — It's — Oh God, I don't remember. Does that make me a slut?

Clarice: Not yet, darling. But you're showing terrific potential.

We join Kate in Hell.

Kate: So then I was on streetcar, speeding towards the entrance of Hell. I hid behind a seat and jumped off before I got there, so I wouldn't get caught. It went off towards the entrance. It was a big entrance, like Disneyland, with lots of turnstiles. Most people got hustled through, but then, somebody went through the metal detector thing and bells and whistles went off and balloons fell like he's the one-trillionth customer or something. The demons were all happy and I saw Satan jump and clap like a little girl, because that's what he was just then. A little girl with Ernest Borgnine's head growing out of her torso. But when Satan's happy, you don't want to be the one doing it for him. When Satan's happy it means that somebody is going to the bad Hell. The bad Hell is bad. I know. I checked.

You don't get there on a streetcar. You get there through a meat grinder. Once you're spit out at the bottom, and then, it gets bad. I saw a hanging cluster of terrorists being filled with molten lead. The lead sort of pisses out of them and all over a pile of U.S. presidents. Reagan's chair has these ass spikes and his scrotum is full of bees. There's even spots for the presidents who aren't dead yet. The Bushes' chairs look goddamn awful. The only VP in the group? Cheney. Good for him, right? Just then I saw the demon working the door. He was kind of a snake demon, and he had just finished shedding a layer of skin. He kicked off the last of it and went off to buff himself or something. I put on his old skin, and did my best demon walk, straight for the door.

At the Pronto Video Awards.

Esther: Me and Clarice drank a couple shots real quick and went to our table because the show was starting. Our table was really near the front since I was with Clarice and it was quite neat to see everybody. The professional awards were first. There was one for best direction and one for best lighting and one for the best use of a warm-blooded animal and the least offensive use of a dwarf. Then finally the amateur awards came up. It was a new category and since there were no directors and that, there were only the performer categories. The one for the best male performer went to this guy who had a handle-bar moustache and huge biceps. He looked really happy and I was happy for him too. Then my award came up and they showed the little clips of the films the people made, and I turned really red. I mean, it's one thing to think that people are watching it in their homes, but I didn't want people looking at it with me here and all. Not that they showed total sex parts, just parts sort of before or, uh, after, you know, kind of tasteful. And I saw mine and I thought, I look like a librarian. And then I took off my glasses and took down my hair and then I looked like a sexpot. Who knew? People like a sexy librarian. Then there was that moment before they read who won and you know, they pause a bit to take the thing out of the envelope and that moment just lasts forever. You just want them to say your name really really bad. So when they said —

Announcer: Esther Star!

Esther: I said — "Oh my god oh my god oh my god oh my god YES YES YES!"

She turns to the audience.

Even though in the long run it would be better if I hadn't won. Because the very next night, this was me on the six o'clock news —

A spotlight hits her.

I want to thank all you excellent people out there for making these movies for people to watch with their girlfriends or boyfriends or even just by themselves for masturbating. Because if it turns you on to watch videos before sex, you should have lots to choose from. And I'd like to thank Clarice and you there, the guy, you know who you are, but mostly I'd like to thank . . . my Mom.

The spotlight goes out.

And my Mom was reached for comment and she said:

Sharon: Well — liberal media elite, gay agenda slander, sexism . . . oh! Oh no!

Sharon vomits.

Esther: But I didn't know any of that at the time. I just knew that I won and I had a new famous friend and tonight was gonna be a good night and then that song came on! And we did, me and Clarice. We drank and danced and I met a really nice dwarf, which I now know like to be called "little people." Those guys are nice. If you get the chance, get to know one, because a lot of people don't bother, I think and it's too bad. The bed was spinning when I finally lay down, and Clarice lay down next to me and the spinning seemed to stop. She inched forward and gave me a small, shy kiss. And I'm not saying what happened next, because it's none of your business.

We join Kate in Hell.

Kate: So I'm inside a demon skin, heading for the door. It stinks like hell, but nobody is stopping me. Once I get through the turnstiles I'm swimming upstream through a sea of the damned. Everybody is crying and praying and apologizing to God. It's enough to break your heart, if you aren't used to it. Luckily, I am. Finally I got through to a door in the back and squeezed through.

And then, I was in this hall of doors. Like, hundreds and hundreds. They were all labeled with symbols and words I couldn't read. I had no idea, so I just picked one. I opened a door with a dragon head on it, and as I did I began to feel like I was every living thing. Like I was a grasshopper and a cabbage and a cow and a Republican and everything else. Like the old hot dog vendor joke. Somebody made me one with everything. Too much for me.

So I shut that door and went to another one with Valkyrie on it. I looked inside and there were Vikings everywhere.

It was a big rustic Viking bar with drunk people fighting. Too much like Georgia. There was this other door, labeled Ron Pederson, and as soon as I opened it up two hot girls tried to blow me while a butler stood by to feed me vodka and sodas. Crazy. There's a million heavens, but Hell is just a big mall.

Then there was a door with a cross on it. Here was my chance to see where Mom was dragging us to. See if Heaven deserves the name. At first it was just clouds and all, but soon the clouds gave way to these little neighbourhoods and all the houses looked the same. And all the men wore these light-coloured suits and all the women were in modest flower print dresses. I know Christians when I see them, and these were them. I just walked and walked. It was always a nice temperature so I never got cold and I didn't eat anymore, so the only problem was that I got bored. Hell sucks and all, but there's lots to do. I wanted to watch TV or go to a movie, but they didn't have any, so I just followed everybody to church. The churches looked like all the churches on earth, but there were no hymnals, because in Heaven, everybody knows the words. Then the preacher came in at the front and it was either Jesus or a guy who looked just like him. He was the first guy I had seen with long hair, because everybody else had these kinda dorky little haircuts. My first thought was that maybe all the preachers dressed up like Jesus, you know, like Vegas and Elvis. But this guy looked right at me and no one else had. Then He clapped his hands and everybody froze, so by then I was convinced.

Jesus: You're not from around here.

Kate: No. I'm not. Are you gonna send me back?

Jesus: Of course not. I was against that place from the beginning. But you know how Dad gets.

Kate: Huh. What am I gonna do now?

Jesus: Come with me.

Kate: And he took my hand and we were suddenly in his apartment.

The lights become wide and bright.

It was a nice place. I mean, really nice. It was huge and had a great view and everything. He took me to a phone and he said –

Jesus: Is there anybody you can call? You know, somebody you could stay with for a while? Until I can work something out?

Kate: I could call my sister.

Jesus: Esther. Good idea. Here's the phone. You might have to call a few times to get through.

Kate: He showed me his phone and I dialed. It took the longest time to get through.

Esther: You know how you never know what is inside someone's head? Like, you might know them real well your whole life and never know that they suffer from schizophrenia? Well, it's really sad when that happens, especially to your Mom. I'm piecing this together from interviews later, but it seems like inside my Mom's head, it went a little like this:

Sarah Palin: Well, isn't this a French tickler on a catfish?

Sharon: Sarah Palin? Is that you?

Sarah Palin: Well, of course it's me, ya silly willy. I wouldn't desert ya in your hour of need.

Sharon: The Democrats are more powerful than ever!

Sarah Palin: It's a tough time for the servants of God. The devil's wearing a short dress, high-kicking all over creation.

Sharon: You could still run for president!

Sarah Palin: Not now. Now, my biggest supporter has a lesbian porn star daughter.

Sharon: It's all her fault. Esther ruined everything! She ruined it with her gayness!

Sarah Palin: Well, you know what I always say. You get that enemy in your sights. And you do not retreat. You reload. You get my meanin', puddin-pop?

Sharon loads a gun.

Sharon: Yes. Yes I do.

We hear a suspenseful sting. We join Esther at the hotel the next morning.

Esther: But I didn't know any of that either! I just woke up so happy. You know sometimes when you wake up happy, but then you remember your life, and then you aren't anymore? Well, it was like that, but when I remembered my life, it just made me happier. I love Clarice! Me and Clarice talked about it and Clarice said I could sleep with guys when I wanted, but it's hard to imagine. We decided we were going to hang out every day, forever, and that's that.

I went down to get the papers, because Clarice said she did the crossword with a pen and I wanted to see. So there I was in the little store they have in the lobby of the hotel. And there I was! I mean, there I was in my slippers, but also there I was on the front page. *San Francisco Chronicle! The Daily News! The New York Times!* All of them had pictures of me. Me with a statue. Me with Clarice. Me with my head on Sharon Stone's body. And the headlines. Sharon Kirkenchuck's Daughter Lesbian Porn Star. Sharon Kirkenchuck's Show Loses Advertisers After Daughter's Porn and Pot Party. And then as if my surprise cup didn't already runneth over. I look up and there's my Mom.

Sharon is unhinged.

Sharon: You've been a very bad girl, Esther. A very bad girl.

Esther: Hi, Mom.

Sharon: Evil comes home to roost, Esther. If you are going to do evil, evil will come, not only to you but to those you say you love.

Esther: I don't just say I love you. I do love you.

Sharon: If you love me, you'll come with me right now.

Esther: And she held out her hand and waited for me to take it. So I asked where we were going and she said:

Sharon: The Shady Acres Rest and Rehabilitation Centre.

Esther: I knew what that was. It was a home where Christian parents could send their gay kids and they would get electro-shocked and drugged and taken to baseball games to make them not gay anymore. I wasn't even a lesbian porn star when she told me about it and I knew even then, no way, nohow, not on a cold day in Hell was I ever going there. But there was my Mom with her hand out and I had never not taken my Mom's hand ever in my whole life. There was about to be a first time for everything when Clarice came up behind me.

Clarice: Well, look at this. I had hoped this would wait until Christmas. Mrs. Kirkenchuck, you've got a lovely daughter.

Esther: It wasn't the wrong thing to say exactly, but it didn't seem to be the right one either, because that vein in her forehead started pumping in a way I hadn't seen since they stopped saying the Lord's Prayer at school. I looked back at Clarice to shut her up and I saw her eyes go wide. I looked back and saw why.

Sharon pulls out her gun.

Sharon: Esther, you are coming with me right now. You are my daughter, my flesh, and I will not see you abandon yourself to this perversity, this lesbianism, this pornography, and this miscreant who has dragged you into it. Come on, right now.

Esther: And no one was more surprised than me when I said, "No. No way. Nohow. I'm happy where I am. I'll live how I want. No. No. No." And I waited for I don't know what. I didn't think my Mom would shoot me, but I didn't think she'd pull a gun on me either. Live and learn, huh? My Mom started screaming and the gun came up and Mom started shooting. She shot a chandelier and a stuffed bear. She shot a window and a stack of newspapers, and then she shot Clarice. When I looked back at Mom, she had stopped to reload, and that's when she got tackled by the busboy. I ran to Clarice.

Clarice: Last week I might have just gone ahead and died. But my mood has improved.

Esther: And then paramedics came. I was really worried. Clarice was already really hungover, so it was terrible timing for getting shot. And it was Mom who had to go to the special home, because as it turns out, shooting people was worse than being a lesbian. She got lots of support in the mail and now there's a website just for her and it gets lots of hits every day from the Christians who think she did the right thing and it was just too bad Clarice didn't die.

Fuck them, I say.

I went home to Elbow, just to pack. I couldn't stay there, now that I was a famous lesbian porn star whose Mom had shot her girlfriend. I was world famous. Already there was hate mail in my mailbox, and a letter from a guy who wanted me to mail him my panties, and some guys yelled stuff at me from pickup trucks. I was sad to leave, because I knew I wouldn't be back. I was someone else now. My Mom said on TV that she would always love me, but she could never accept me. So, with Dad disappeared wherever and Kate gone, that meant I had no more family to speak of. Not in Saskatchewan or anywhere. So, I'm moving to California. My videos, seems we made, uh, forty or so, they're all selling real well, especially now.

I keep hearing from people at Pronto. They want to make some more movies, but I don't think I'd be very good if I knew there was a camera there. I'm not really a porn star. I just play one, on some computers. But it's nice to have all this money coming in, plus the job Clarice gave me, and the book Clarice is gonna help me write of this story I'm telling right now, and I think living in San Francisco will be really fun.

I'd be happy, like, what did my Grandpa say, like a pig in poop! Except for not having any family. And even though Mom would just call up and talk about God and politics, she was still my Mom. I guess even though I'm a lesbian porn star, I still have family values. So, umm, that's it, I guess. That's the whole story. Esther Kirkenchuck. Research Assistant to Clarice DuBois. Elbow, Saskatchewan. Saying goodbye to her little house. Her little town. Her little life.

She turns off the recorder. The phone rings.

Esther: Hello? . . . Oh come on. That's gross okay, my sister is dead . . . Wait a second? Wait for what?

Kate appears before her.

Esther: Oh my God. Kate, are you a ghost?

Kate: Yeah, I think so. Can I stay with you for a while?

Esther: I'm moving to San Francisco.

Kate: Well, can I come? I don't take up much room and I only eat sunlight. It's just until I can reincarnate. But that could be awhile.

Esther: Of course you can come with me.

Kate: Thanks. So what's been going on?

Esther: A lot. A whole lot.

Kate: Are you crying?

Esther: I just really missed you. I really really missed you.

Esther touches her.

Esther: You tingle.

Kate: Yeah.

Esther: It's crazy.

Esther touches her a couple more times. They giggle. Blackout.

THE END

MOVING ALONG

PRODUCTION HISTORY

Moving Along was commissioned by Theatre of the New Heart, for their site-specific theatre series. The first production took place in 2000 in the basement of Sophie Lees' rented house on Stony Plain Road and 126 Street in Edmonton, Alberta. The audience capacity was thirty.

Starring: Chris Craddock
Directed by: Sophie Lees
Chair Designed and Built By: Doug Field, based on a concept by Chris Craddock

Since its premiere, it has been performed at festivals across Canada, as well as appearing during theatre seasons at Theatre Network and One Yellow Rabbit.

PRODUCTION NOTE

The electro-chair (as I have come to call it) is a chair specifically designed for this show, with dimmers sunk into the arms, leading to outlets. The outlets have a variety of lights plugged into them, all facing the actor in the chair. The actor controls the lighting design from the stage as he performs his show. This chair was created to solve two problems:

(1) Theatre lights are expensive and left in the control of people who may or may not care about your show.

(2) Theatre lights are slow. They take some fraction of a second to hum up to light and that is too slow for this show.

The electro-chair provides a ready-to-travel set and lighting rig that can be placed anywhere with electricity and an audience, and is in full control of the performing artist, thus removing the need for a stage manager.

A NOTE ON THE SCRIPT

The modular nature of *Moving Along* means that it can and will be updated as I live on through my life. This is the definitive version at the time of publication, but may not be exactly the same as the show you see when I do it again.

And I will do it again.

When reading, please accept a paragraph break as a lighting cue, but there are lots inside the paragraphs as well, too many to list.

The stage contains only the "electro-chair" and a bottle of water.

The actor enters in a suit and tie, wearing no shoes. He sits in the chair and stretches his neck and prepares to perform. He takes a long drink from the water bottle and then throws it away. He shuts off the lights, and then turns them all on quickly, as if just now discovering the presence of the audience.

Oh! You must be here about the collection.

Moving along.

I was sitting in the men's room of a greasy spoon the other day. I was sitting there and I was having bacon and eggs, well, not in the men's room, but in the diner proper, which is step two in my "How to Get Over A Hangover Procedure" after the hot shower, but before the joint. I was sitting there in this men's room which was a less-than-charming place, believe you me, and I was about to dismiss it, you know, *aesthetically,* but then I noticed this –

hand-painted tile on the wall.

The old tile had been broken by a drunk or something and had been replaced by this –

hand-painted tile! –

– that depicted a . . . boy with a barrow, or a rampant eagle, or, like, an old lady kissing another old lady – okay, I forget what it was! But it was beautiful! And it was the only one like it in the room! And it occurred to me then, that I could go about and break every single tile in this place and maybe each one of them would be so –

Fabulously replaced!

And then this greasy spoon would have the most amazing men's room of any greasy spoon in Canada, possibly *North America!*

But then I thought, No. They wouldn't thank me for that. No one appreciates damage. At the time.

Moving along.

The performer screams as if waking from a nightmare.

OH! Pardon me! I had one of those mornings, you know, one of those mornings where you sleep in and you rush through the early part of the day? Well, I had one of *those* mornings, and I must have been in quite a hurry, because I got all the way to school and I was sitting there in class before I realized I had forgotten to put on my pants! No pants! No underwear either. I was just sitting there in a shirt and jacket and the bottom half of my body was just naked, just floppy and naked. And just as I noticed, everyone else noticed too, and boy did they *laugh*. I mean I deserved it –

The performer indicates his nudity.

I guess! But it wasn't regular sort of laughing; it was kind of a weird kind that distorts the faces kind of a –

HAHAHAHAHAHAHAHAHAHAHAHAHA!

It's a terrible situation to be in and I recommend you avoid it, if you can. But you can't. But there's *worse*.

Last week I found myself in this abandoned house, this huge, cobwebbed house, wandering, and suddenly I think to myself:

Fuck me. There is a monster in this house.

And I know, the way I know things in *situations*, that the monster wants to eat me completely, bones and all and to lick up all the blood and it will be as if I never existed at all.

And just as I'm knowing it, just as the thought is hanging in my head –

There's the monster. Hanging above me. And I try to scream but nothing comes out.

The performer backlights and lets out a weak scream, like a dreamer in a nightmare, who calls for help but cannot be heard.

And then the monster turns from one monster into a group of monster dogs!

The better to eat me with –

And then, then I feel them take hold of my limbs! I feel their jaws on my arms and legs! And they eat me and I'm gone.

Forever.

Gone.

These are terrible situations to be in, and you know, when I was a younger man, younger than this, well, a pre-teen, let's not mince words, I mean . . .

I was a child.

The performer sighs as though deeply ashamed.

When I was a child, I was in a situation like this every time I turned around! It's one of the most attractive aspects of growing up. That, and freedom, and power, and . . . all the pie you want. When you grow up, your imagination recedes somewhat, you believe in things less and you sleep better. I often sleep right through the night these days. And I hardly ever require changing.

Moving along.

I'd, uh, I'd like to have a moment of silence, please, for someone who was very close to me, very, very close to me. Please, just a moment for . . . Arthur Fonzarelli. For the Fonz.

The performer does a "thumbs-up" as the lights float down.

Ayyyyyyyyyyy!

What a guy, the Fonz! I mean, he had superpowers, sure, but that was the least of it! I mean, what was *fonzie* about the Fonz was the way he would approach each situation with this unperturbed air, this kind of preternatural calm, that later became known as —

Cool.

Fonzie was cool, plus he had low-level telekinesis that he could do stuff with, you know? Like starting cars!

He starts a car.

Making the jukebox go, but that stuff was just for fun! It was just for show! Because Fonzie's real power . . . was with the *ladies*.

You see, Fonzie gave off a *pheromone* that would cause women to just throw themselves at him! Two, three at a time! With no sense of competition, no expectation of commitment. Women didn't need commitment from him. No! It was understood that he was the Fonz, and that was not his way!

Damn! Fonzie was cool!

And his influence on me, personally, is hard to calculate, heh heh. In 1979, Fonzie appeared on *Sesame Street*, and told me it was important I brush my teeth.

I brushed my teeth five times a day for three weeks! But that's just the tip of the iceberg! I mean, what Fonzie truly taught me was, is that it is important . . . no, *vital!* To date as many women as possible! And to kiss them! To kiss them all! Fonzie's Fonzie's lips –

The performer is overcome with emotion.

I – I – I'm, I'm sorry! Please, could we do that thing where we m-m-move along?

The performer sees the lights are unchanged.

PLEASE COULD WE –

Moving along.

In childhood I was polite, and well-mannered, so I'm told. I said *please* and *thank you* and took seriously my mother's wish that I *clean my plate*. I did misbehave, of course, but my misbehaviours took the shape of funny little anecdotes that showed I was more spirited than bad.

Uh . . . for example I, I took my crayons to the TV set 'cause the set was a black and white, and I wanted a colour one!

I sawed the legs off the coffee table to make it more hospitable for my baby sister.

I blew up the fire station because the man in the oxygen mask scared me!

You see, in childhood, your eyes are *larger*. So you're rarely perceived as *evil*.

Teens, however . . .

Teens are full of dark secrets, hopes and fears, and pustules and excretions, and they aren't as cute as they used to be or as striking as they will become. They are the scary in-between creatures. And though they scare everyone, they scare their parents the most. Because it is their job to control them and they simply . . . cannot.

And the harder they try, the worse it is.

For example! When I was fifteen, I would often look in the personal ads in the back of the *Edmonton Sun*. There was always a "man seeking a man" in those pages. "Man seeking man slim handsome 18 to 35." And even though I was only fifteen, I felt sure I would do. I also felt sure, instinctively sure, for I had no experience at all with these things, at the time. I knew that if I could find the placer of this ad, I could receive *proficient* and *enthusiastic* ORAL SEX!

Which seemed to me at fifteen to be a kind of Xanadu, available only to porn stars, Hugh Hefner, and the members of Mötley Crüe.

But I had no phone of my own and I must assume the man found another slim, handsome man or maybe he didn't find one or at least not the right one because you still see the ads today . . .

The performer feels sheepish and lowers the lights.

Moving along.

A little secret about myself. It seems that I have the *Force*. Yeah, it seems my father as well as being a pipefitter was also quite a powerful *Jedi* and it's hereditary, somewhat. As it turns out I have it too.

The performer puts on a Darth Vader voice.

The Force is strong with this one.

And back to normal.

That's what they tell me. And it's funny, you know, because I'm not the kind to rush out and join some *rebel alliance*, you know? I mean, I vote for the Green Party, but that's about it. So I use my powers for little things. Like turning out the lights when I'm already in bed. Reaching things that are too high for me. Lightsaber fights.

I mean, it would be great to have some kind of purpose! Some big, noble thing I could throw myself into. And there are things I could do, I suppose. I could be more involved in the political life of my community. I could sponsor a child from an underprivileged country! I could dig wells . . . in some country . . . that's *dry*.

But I'm not about to join an illegal *militia*. Some rebel army that's bent on overthrowing the government, no matter what kind of *Force* I might be wielding! I mean:

Fuck that!

A guy could get *killed*.

And it's not that I'm for the *Empire*. It's just that, you know . . . I'm busy.

There's this work I gotta do! There's dishes in my sink! There's a show on I like! There's a new superhero movie coming out! I'm hungry! I'm thirsty! I'm bored! I'm jealous! I'm sitting uncomfortably! That light is too bright! I have shooting pains in my chest and left arm! I wish I had a million dollars! I wish I could fly . . .

With a change in the lights, the performer flies.

You see, I want more of . . . I need less of . . . What I'd always imagined for myself . . . for me . . .

The performer looks out at the audience, embarrassed by his selfishness.

When I went to university, I decided to join a fraternity. This in and of itself was a strange decision. I was not a jockish type, not going into business, was not a *joiner* by any means. But I had gotten it into my head that joining a frat was a rich kid thing to do and no way was I going to let being a poor kid keep me from a rich kid experience!

Plus, I had a best friend who was dragging me to stuff, and it was fun. Plus, the frat did nice things, played with some kids from a shelter or something, and had a code of gentlemanly conduct, which was clearly *not upheld* but I liked the idea of.

So, for all these reasons, I joined a fraternity. Delta Kappa Epsilon. The infamous *Dekes*. All year long I worked hard with my pledge brothers and finally won the right to be "initiated." And this is what I want to tell you about tonight. The details are fuzzy, but it was the only initiation ritual ever offered me as a young man, and I made a blood oath that I would not reveal it. I'm breaking that oath tonight, and I don't feel guilty, because that promise was extracted under extreme duress.

So we show up at the house with the stuff we were supposed to bring. A couple changes of clothes, eggs, bacon, loaves of bread, beer, and a homemade wooden paddle.

We show up and we start to clean the house. There's older guys there, alumni, and they yell at us while we clean. And then we drink. And we drink and drink and drink until we eventually pass out.

And then, very shortly after, we are woken up. There's more yelling now. It's time to wake up and put on your exercise clothes. But you can't find them and there's yelling and soon you wind up standing in the backyard in winter with two mismatched shoes. And then you run. You're hungover, maybe you're still drunk, but you run and run.

The jocks appear, truly fit young men, which you are not, fresh and well rested, which you are not. And they take you to a parking garage and run you up and down the stairs. Up and down the hill. All around, and they yell and yell.

And we do this for hours.

And then you get back to the house. And you cook up the bacon and the eggs. We sneak some of the eggs into our own mouths and it's a good thing too, because this meal is not for us. We're going in the box.

So we all go into the box. It's a big plywood box set up in a common room, and we all pile into it, like we're ready to be human trafficked. And then they shout and bang on the box with the paddles they have. The paddles they must've made and brought here, just like you made and brought yours.

And you do laps through the house. But you can't go through a door frontwards. No! It's a rule. You have to go through doors backwards. So you're running and spinning through these doors and then everyone back in the box.

Then at some point, we are told we are going to a fancy dinner! This is great news, because we're all really hungry. So we all troop naked through the shower, spinning through all the doors. We have a brief cold shower, and then we put on our nice clothes. We're blindfolded and put into a truck. When the blindfolds come off, we are not at a fancy dinner. We're in a warehouse! And the meal is a collection of fun gross fun things they thought up to serve us! Like cat food! And Jell-O made with vinegar! And we are told that we cannot puke. For if we puke, we must *eat it*. And "eat it" is a phrase we hear a lot at this point. Fratboys screaming at their fellow fratboys:

EAT IT!

EAT IT!

And you take what gaggy bites you may and then we're all blindfolded again and put back in the truck and taken back to the house. And now it's time for the games.

"The games" means that you get in a circle, and you have a number. When your number is called, you jump forward that number of times and you await instructions. You might be asked about the history of the brotherhood, or made to do push-ups. And now there is a new rule. You may not refer to yourself as "I." You must refer to yourself as "it." As in —

Sir, it has to go to the bathroom, sir!

or

Sir, it doesn't know the answer, sir!

And we do this for hours.

Then they sit us in chairs in the basement, all blindfolded, with this bizarre music blaring. And then make us hold our paddles out with our arms so we don't go to sleep. And one by one we get pulled out of there, and we face the tribunal!

The tribunal is three older guys that you know from the frat, who sit there in druid robes, right? Three little Ben Kenobis sitting there, and they ask you questions about the frat that you couldn't answer even you had eaten or slept the last two days, and during one of these sessions we sign in blood!

They have a big scary knife they show you, but then in the end they use this little thing for diabetics, just poke! And you smear your blood on this paper, and then you've signed in blood and you go back to the basement to hold up your paddle.

And we do this for hours.

And then we're taken downtown to the Masons' temple. The Masons really *get us*, you know? And they let us use their pad. You sit in there for a long time, while someone plays the theme from *The Exorcist* on a piano they have there. And then, the blindfold comes off. Now you face a huge panel of guys in Jedi robes. All the older guys you know from the frat.

You figure, this is it. You did it.

But they tell you that you didn't do it, in fact. In fact you *failed*. You failed at being initiated so badly, that not only are you not going to be a *Deke*, but your big brother, in my case the guy who got me into this, your big brother was going to be stripped of rank too. You let him down. You let the brotherhood down. You let yourself down. All of this was for nothing. And they tell us all this. And we're so tired and hungry that we believe them. And we cry. We cry and cry into our laughing brothers' shoulders until the time is come to reveal . . . Psych! Just kidding! You got in after all.

And we get to eat. And we get to go home. And we sleep for, in my case, like, eighteen hours. And when we wake up, we feel amazing. We survived something. We feel like we joined more than a silly after-school drinking and womanizing club. We became *Men*. These guys who put us through it, are not *abusive assholes*. They're our *brothers*. And you may not even like half of them, but they went through that same crazy, awful thing you did, and that's enough for you, when you're twenty.

I guess if it had been external, a real thing, like a war, it might have bonded us forever. But we did it to ourselves. And now, it's just a thing that happened. All those years ago.

Moving along.

When I was twelve, my father took me to a cattle auction. We would often go to things like that together on our every second weekend out of nostalgia for his rural upbringing which, um, he didn't seem to like. It didn't seem very good for him and judging from the stories it seemed to consist largely of being locked in the trunks of various stockcars by his older brothers!

But anyway, there we were at this cattle auction and guys in John Deere caps would trundle out these harried and bewildered calves and we would bid on them. We saw three or so before Dad found one that he really liked, based on criteria that, I don't know.

I guess it just had that special *something*.

So we bid on it and won. We bought it. We owned it. We could do with it what we pleased! And what we pleased to do with it, was stuff it in the back of my grandma's station wagon, and take it to my uncle's farm.

I rode in the back with the calf. It sucked on my fingers and got snot on my hands. I was a real live cowboy!

So we got it to the farm and we put it in the barn and you know, I *tried* to play with it for a while. But cows aren't that much fun to play with! Not even the puppies! I mean they won't catch anything! They won't chase anything! And they have too many pointy bits to effectively cuddle. So I said –

Bye.

And I went back to the city. Got back to my life. I think there was a Lego set that was taking up a lot of my time. And I pretty much forgot about him.

I heard he was sick once, and costing money. Maybe more money than he was worth! And that touched a nerve, because I think we all worry about costing more than we're worth. And another couple of seasons went by and I was visiting my dad again and I noticed . . .

There were lots of packages of meat in the freezer. I, I thought about it for a minute in the middle of my burger.

The performer freezes, staring at his burger.

I thought about how young and vulnerable he was and how he sucked on my finger that day.

But I guess I didn't particularly love that little cow. Because I didn't scream or run away or become a vegetarian. No, I paused.

Pause. The performer stares at his burger again.

And then I went right back to eating. And uh, you know . . .

He was good.

Moving along.

Just a side note!

The performer uses the backlight now, pulsing it with his voice.

For fun right now, let's all try to think of the first thing we remember. Fight through the fog of childhood. The hiding. The crying. Struggle through all that, and try to find that first shred of memory. The memory you didn't understand at the time. The one you reordered and reinterpreted later. Your first memory.

He moves his head and the backlight glares at the audience.

Everybody's shy so I'll go first.

I'm riding my white horse. I'm riding it and I'm chasing a dinosaur through the streets of an ancient city. And even though I'm the one doing the chasing, I'm the one escaping. Or trying to. Because I'm sitting on my white wooden rocking horse, I'm sitting on it, and there are some strange men here. They're tall and they wear uniforms like I've seen on TV, and one of them looks at me like he's sorry. He's so sorry, and Mom's crying and there's been shouting and that's why they're here, and they're sorry, and Mom's sorry and everybody's sorry and that's how it is. And I'm three.

They were policemen, those men. They're looking for my father. Because him and Mom used to fight. Loudly. Violently. Neighbours noticed, called for peace. If not peace then —

Quiet.

The performer distances himself by becoming an expert.

You see, we become fertile too young for our society! It leads to shame, and poverty, and police calling and all sorts of problems! We're just too darn fertile!

But radiation levels are increasing all the time so let's hope for the best.

That's a nice thought, isn't it? "Let's hope for the best."

Nah, that's not quite it, is it?

Let's hope *we* get the best.

Noooo –

Let's hope! We get *lots* and *lots* . . . of the best. Yeah, that's what I'm fucking talking about.

Moving along.

I had, well, *have* this Uncle Phillip. Funny little guy, Uncle Phillip, worked in a bank, all his life. He has two condominiums and a Jaguar he drives twice a year, but he dries his dishes with tattered rags because he can't stand the expense of new tea towels! Well, he's never seen a woman naked in all his life, it seems to me, and I always kind of thought he was queer. But there's this problem of him being such a terrible dresser, and I couldn't settle the tension in my mind. So one day I was talking to my pal Devin about my Uncle Phillip and I said:

"You know, Devin, my Uncle Phillip? I always thought he was at least a little bit gay. For lots of reasons, not least of all that he was a fantastic swimmer."

And Devin said, "Oh, he swam."

And I said, "Yeah."

And Devin said, "Did he wear little shorts?"

And I said, "Well, yeah."

And Devin said, "Did he have a big cock?"

And I said, "Uh . . . well, umm, yeah."

And Devin said, "I think you're the one who's a little bit gay."

And I just smiled. Because I was twenty-four then and I had already had a "relationship."

Moving along.

My mother found religion when I was still quite young. There was a pair of plaid pants that I had to wear to Sunday School, and I blame the tightness and the itchiness of those pants for the state of my spiritual decay today. Anyhow, my Mom was religious! And she gets more religious as she goes on. Like a spiritual snowball rolling down a mountain of Jesus!

Jesus. She loves that guy.

She gives ten percent of the family income to the man from Galilee, and every month she picks a different bill to *not pay* so that ends can meet. But she's a cheerful lady, though her self-esteem's not what I wish it was. I mean, she worries she's stupid, and she *is not*. But like I say, she's *cheerful*.

But there was this one morning she was beyond cheerful, okay? She was ecstatic! She was hopping about singing a little song and my stepfather came in and he was looking sleepy, and sheepish. And Mom asked him for something and he said, "No." And she said, "But you got something you wanted *last night*."

Then I knew.

In my eleven-year-old head. Mom had sex. She got *some.*

And it made all the difference in the world! She was happier than I'd ever seen her! She was thrilled! Life was rich and new for her! A shiny thing! A bright toy of a life was hers! And all because she had gotten laid.

I always suspected that sex was the key to happiness and here was irrefutable evidence.

I was so happy for her. So happy for me! I was sure everything was going to be *so different* now! No more itchy pants church! No more forbidden devil music! No more don't do this, don't watch that! It was all giggles and cheesecake from here to puberty, and I would be phoning in the rest of my childhood because MY MOM GOT LAID!

But, um, the next night, she didn't get . . . or something. Because things pretty much went back to normal.

Moving along.

Just a side note.

Have you ever been with someone who just seems to steal all your spark? I mean they don't even seem to mean to, but there you are with all your thoughts and innovations burning in your head, but you're too intimidated somehow to bring them to the fore. So you say nothing. And the person you're with assumes you're stupid. And you start to feel stupid. And they start to make you feel stupid. And you don't think this is fair, because you're not stupid, and you know it, but you never told them you're not stupid, so you have no one to blame but yourself?

Moving along.

There's been a lot of speculation, mostly on the internet, as to whether or not gay men have bigger penises than straight men. Some experts say this has something to do with a gay gene and this speaks to evolution and this makes me wonder. Just who exactly is out there *proliferating* this gay gene? Gay men are not known for their predilection for procreation. Lesbians do it more often because, well, they can. But for the most part, breeders breed and gay folk make fabulous aunts and uncles. But. You'll also hear about those folks who get married, and have a couple of kids and then show up in a sailor suit to the company Christmas party. And maybe these are the people who are responsible for the evolution of homos, on a strictly Darwinian basis. Maybe every time a lesbian and a gay man inexplicably find themselves beginning a family together, maybe then the gay gene meets the gay gene and cocks get bigger all over the world! Maybe more than that, maybe for women the gay gene is building a mightier clitoris, bigger, stronger, faster, more responsive, able to be engorged with more hot blood, and able to cause multiple orgasms with a single lick!

Maybe we all owe a twisted debt to repression.

Maybe not.

One man, a *famous* man, said to me that gay men masturbate more. They masturbate more, at that crucial time in adolescence when all the cock-growing hormones are present and looking for a clue on just how far to go. I find this comforting because I'd like to think I spent that time improving myself.

Moving along.

Just a side note.

A lot of young lads, more than you might think, are just getting into puberty when they notice that they have this swelling in their chest, these little breasts perk up. Just when they're starting to fit the man suit they're supposed to wear from here on in, they grow these little *breasts*. Which are part of a hormone imbalance, part of having too much estrogen when you're a boy and not a girl. This happens to very obese youngsters more often than not, these —

The performer switches to the expert, suddenly furious.

FAT LITTLE BOYS! Just when they're developing their sense of humour or their computer skills —

The performer switches back to normal.

Just when perhaps they've finally found the thing that will allow them to be fat and still make their way, their body *fucks them over!*

And it grows these breasts. And I ought to know because it happened, to —

a friend of mine.

This friend of mine was perhaps meant to be the fattest of fat boys instead of the merely husky one that he was. You see he turned ten in 1982 when the fitness craze was at its genesis and they started to show *Rocky* on TV. He was ten years old and already thoroughly disenchanted with this body of his, as compared to the ones on TV. And he thought a lot about how great it would be to have a goal, like Rocky, some big important thing that you wanted so bad that you would chase chickens all day, and turn your body from a bad useless one into a good violent one. So he did push-ups in front of Rocky from *Rocky*. He did sit-ups in front of Leroy from *Fame*. He thwarted his destiny and heroically attained what was still a below-average body. So when my, *his* mother presented him to a surgeon, the surgeon expected to see an obese boy with tiny little girl breasts. He instead saw a merely husky boy with tiny little girl breasts. He shook my friend's hand and went right to work.

Probably surgeons think a lot about their handshake because people are supposed to trust them and, more importantly, their hands.

Then my friend's right arm got very cold, he went to sleep and he woke up again, in the presence of bandages and the absence of breasts. And as soon as he could, he got right back to the gym and went right back to work on creating that acceptable body. I remember lies he told people later, at the swimming pool and other places to explain the bandages and later the scars on his chest. He told some friends of mine that he was in a car accident. Yeah! That he got hit by a car, rolled up on the hood, smacked the windshield! Cracking a few ribs. He told this girl that he had gotten into a knife fight, that his enemy had two knives and had sliced him just, so.

He's an honest man, but he was not an honest kid. And having breasts is definitely the kind of thing a fourteen-year-old boy lies about. It's worse than liking WHAM!

And Duran Duran, which we also secretly did.

But later on the scars faded and his chest hair grew in and he didn't have to lie any more.

Except about the WHAM!

This just in.

Your loved ones are getting ready to leave you. Right now. And you them. Already your bodies are giving out their almost last bits of themselves, and how many more times are you going to do all the things that you like to do? Before you're gone.

Or they are.

How Much Do You Get?

That's the question we're looking in the horoscopes for!

How many walks in the park are you going on? How many beautiful people are going to offer themselves to you? How many nights will you drink too much and do something just crazy? How many times will you laugh, and laugh and laugh? How many times will you look around the room at the people in it and feel completely accepted and loved? How many roller coasters will you ride? How many times will you dream of flying? How many times will your heart swell with love and excitement? How many times will you say:

Oh my God, this is it! This is so fucking good! This is it! This is it! This! Is! It!

Twenty times?

The performer turns off one of the lights.

Fifty times?

The performer turns off one of the lights.

One hundred times?

The performer turns off one of the lights.

Five hundred times?

The performer turns off the last of the lights.

A thousand seems like too few. Like tragically far, far, far, far too few! A cheat, a theft, a terrible trick played on us all! We should have more, so much more of everything! It isn't fair that we don't get to do it all, so much better and more fully than we do. We should get a million walks in the park! A billion beautiful people should offer themselves to you! You should touch the cheek of your lover and cry with the closeness you share a thousand million, gillion, billion, trillion, *fabrillion* times!

But we don't. And the chances we have, we waste.

On rush hour, on television commercials, on being on hold with Telus. And I don't want to tell you what to do, but whatever you like to do, you should do it. Now. Because no matter how old you are, you are so very quickly running out of time.

Moving along.

My grandmother had the spookiest house. It creeped us all out. It was one of those big farmhouses you see in southern Ontario all the time on a field that's too big for them with a dilapidated barn standing off to the side, like security for a man who is no longer president!

There was this door on the second floor that led to *nowhere!* I now know that it led to a balcony that fell off in, like, nineteen-aught-six, but when I was a kid it was like some kind of scary trap or trick or something. "The Door to Nowhere!"

My grandma sometimes creeped me out too. Even though I loved her, love her. I mean, she's a sweet old lady, but she had this tiny round mustache just under her nose. It was exactly as if a tiny brown spider had been crawling there and she'd squashed it! And then left it there, for forty-five years. But even though she lived in a creepy house and had a brown spider mustache I loved her, love her. She's a sweet old lady and she got us those sweet cereals we never got at home. She stepped on my frog once, but that was an accident. She was just my sweet grandma!

But being a grandma and a mother are two different things and my mother never got the sweet cereals when she was a kid. My Mom had Grandma for her mom and then she was not sweet old Grandma, but mean old *mother!*

And when my Mom turned up pregnant . . .

Grandma locked her in the house. Wouldn't let Dad see her. Wouldn't let Mom come to the phone, until such time that she had extracted a promise of marriage from the seventeen-year-old version of my Dad. Like a shotgun wedding, but with kidnapping!

I've seen the wedding photos and they're surprisingly cordial. I mean, I guess that's just how it was back then.

"You knocked up my daughter! I hate you! Now what are you going to do about it? You will? Welcome to the family!"

And my Mom. She was a babe. Fully a 1972 hottie. And then I came along and . . . ruined her figure.

Moving along.

In 2005, I gave up dating people that I already knew. People I knew were all in theatre and when we broke up it was always this atom bomb going off in the middle of a perfectly pleasant life. But worse, I was sentimental and emotional and impulsive and a drunk, and being my ex-girlfriend in the cozy confines of the Edmonton theatre community was no cakewalk, believe you me. So with all this in mind, I chose to date on the internet, before it was officially totally fine.

And it is now totally fine. If some of you are still thinking it's some kind of nerdy shameful thing, stop it right now. It's fine. Go get some. Seriously.

One caution I will say is that this kind of dating really favours people who can write. All of the early communication is written, so if you're bad at that, I dunno, work out more and hang out at supermarkets.

So, I wasn't sure what to expect from internet dating, but it was totally awesome! I got quickly into a series of pleasant assignations, small, fun, disposable relationships, drama-free, which is just the thing after years of dramatic breakups with real drama *experts*, drama professionals in fact, none more so than myself.

I met most of these women on the "Dating" section of the site. And dating is what we would do. But every so often, I would also meet people in the "Casual Encounters" section! Yeah, you know it! Slutty cousin to the dating section. And this was where I met a particularly cute girl, who was looking for a particularly casual thing, and I thought to myself, yes please!

And that woman . . . turned out to be my wife.

Moving along.

I mentioned before that I had a "relationship" with not-a-woman, as was my wont, but with a *man*.

The performer makes a shocked face.

And showing my usual reckless imprudence, I had a relationship with not some waiter, or biochemistry student, but with a Famous Man. And not just any famous man, but a man who had gained fame in the *very pursuit in which I was engaged*. The problems were immediate and *severe*.

You see, just when I was starting out in my profession, just when I was hungry to be judged for my own spirit and my own merits, just when I wanted my community to hear my name clear like a bell and unblemished like a baby, I was instead:

The famous man's boyfriend.

And that didn't suit me at all.

Also . . .

He wasn't a very nice man for lots of reasons. Most of them stemming from the fact that he was such a famous man. And he worried constantly that people were taking advantage of him, and in all fairness, some of them were.

Moving along.

I remember when I was four, and this is perhaps my second oldest memory. I was at the preschool playing Batman and Robin and a man came up. He gave me a finger puppet and he talked to me for a little while urgently and with great feeling, to show how much he cared for me. And I thought I knew him, he certainly looked familiar to me. I was sure I knew him, I must have known him, because I was very suspicious of strangers. And we played finger puppets for a little while and he was gone.

I've reconstructed that memory in the years to follow and I now realize that, that man was my father.

Moving along.

Just a side note.

Have you ever been walking along, maybe running an errand or something and suddenly you think to yourself:

Fuck me. This isn't my life. I'm in the wrong place, at the wrong time, in an entirely inappropriate *sweater!* I should be welding underwater, I should be in the camel husbandry business, I should be someone else, somewhere else, with entirely different connections to the world.

And then as quickly as it comes up it passes and I continue to the tailors to get my pants hemmed.

Moving along.

If there was one thing I could say to my stepfather. If he were here, though he isn't, I would never let him come to a play with this much swearing.

FUCK!

I would say:

I'm sorry. I'm sorry, sorry for . . . oh, for a million things . . .

For lying to your face that time.

For the statue I broke.

For saying I didn't respect you.

For comparing you to Superman.

For the disaster at the father-son Cub Camp.

I'm sorry. What can I say, I was just another idiot who thought less of you for being thin, and smart.

If there were two things I could say to my stepfather, if he were here right now, though of course he isn't.

FUCK!

I would say also this: Thank you. Thank you. For what? For a million things. But mainly, for taking good care of my Mom.

Moving along.

I remember the first time I went to a play. I was maybe ten years old and my mother took me to this play at this church. It was a play about dying, every character died, and not just at the end, like with Shakespeare, but all the way through. Each vignette featured another character who would die and then either go to Heaven or Hell depending on whether or not they had been saved. And if they had been saved, lights and music and loveliness, and they pranced through the Pearly Gates. But if they were not saved, and many of them weren't, because theatre, in the end, needs to be depressing, if they were not saved, they went to Hell. And the stage turned red and the howling was deafening, it was scary, if you were ten, it was scary to see the people dragged off to Hell.

And I loved it. It was great, committed acting, even better than the Grade Six play at my elementary school. I clapped and clapped, but the show wasn't over yet. Because then, they asked the crowd if there was anyone there who wanted to be saved.

And I wasn't saved yet.

And my Mom looked at me, like –

And I put my hand up. I got up with a few others, and I made my way down to the stage. It felt great, to get up on that stage. I didn't know then if I was joining Christianity or the theatre, but it felt great, whatever it was, it was intoxicating. And I prayed with this young man, this teenager, tall and handsome in a button-down collar shirt. We prayed and I asked Jesus Christ into my heart, and I was saved. And it felt . . . okay. It was nice. Every ten-year-old wants to be in the same club with their mommy, and it felt really good. A few days later, that handsome boy in the button-down collar shirt called me to see how I was doing and that felt good. Being a Christian felt good.

And I started to think like a Christian. A lot of Christians pray for things that are likely to happen anyway and then feel blessed, and I was one of those. I dropped some papers on a windy day and I prayed for the wind to die down, and it *did*. I shyly witnessed to people I knew were Christians already, just to try it out.

Did you know that Jesus loves you?

And they did, and I did too. It was great. But time went on, and I started to develop a sex drive and a political awareness. I began to find out about all the things that weren't allowed, which in my house was a lot. I discovered drugs and booze and many ungodly things and in the end, as good as it felt, I couldn't keep it up. I couldn't stick it out. I wasn't a Christian.

But if you are one, and you can do it, and you don't mind being held responsible for the religious right —

Because I do hold you responsible —

Then, go for it. Keep that feeling. It feels great. To be so *sure*.

But if you're not a Christian, well, I think it's okay to discriminate against them a little bit. Because they aren't born like that, you know.

It's a lifestyle choice.

Moving along.

So we broke up, me and the Famous Man. After nine months of whatever it was. Which is enough to have a baby, but I don't have to tell you, we didn't. He called me over to his house. He gave me a bag with some T-shirts and things in it. He lowered the boom and it was over. And I said:

FUCK YOU!

Not to him in the room, but to him in my head.

And it's hard to believe now, but there was a time when I would repeat it to him, in my head, whenever I happened to think of him, as I went along serving my tables, living my life. And then one day I had a chance to go through the bag he sent me off with and in the bag I found a tape. It was a tape that he had made for me. And as I listened to it I began to realize that every song held a special significance. Held a special message for me about his perception of our relationship. There was that song: "Don't You Want Me Baby"!

"You were working as a waitress in a cocktail bar when I found you!"

It's about a successful man who takes a woman from nowhere, and makes something of her. I'm sure I don't have to cast that little playlet for you! There were pop songs and rock songs and show tunes. One from *Evita*, can you guess which? They were mostly about an innocent being romantically victimized and thus serving to just piss me off.

But there was this one bluesy song that stood out from the bunch. I forget it mostly but the chorus sticks with me and maybe it will stick with you.

The performer switches to the backlight, on low.

"I'm so fucking lonely. And I'm not even high. I'm so fucking lonely. That I think I'm going to die."

The performer looks up. He gets it now and nods a moment. He shrugs it off.

Moving along.

The performer takes up the aspect of the expert.

Hard to believe now –

Perhaps –

But I was once the despised! Untouchable! Of the lowest social caste imaginable! You see, back in junior high, I was a huge dork.

Yeah, I had made some key social blunders, and I was outwardly a heavy metal enthusiast. But my hair didn't look good long, and all the oil from my pubescent face got caught in my peach-fuzzy beard, and my zits were juicy and peaked!

Also, you know, I was eccentric.

Which is weird.

And I was not tough.

Which is wimpy.

And I pissed off a local girl of much influence.

Nadira MacDonald.

I won't say her name –

Nadira MacDonald.

Because she was a terrible person!

Nadira MacDonald.

And I would hate it if anything bad were to happen to her. You know, like, if her house were to burn down?

Ninety-six-eleven Walnut Street.

And she decided that her intramural activity would be to make me miserable because . . .

Volleyball was full.

And she did. I was truly miserable every day. I dreaded going to school every day because everyone was so mean to me there. Old friends deserted me like brokers from a sinking firm. I mean, they had high school to think about, after all, and they couldn't afford loyalty.

And then one summer I went away, and during that summer . . .

I changed.

Yeah, I got a haircut. And I learned to shave and a lot of my zits went away. And I got back into working out, a little bit, like this much. And I got like, uh, three new shirts.

And when I got back to school, nobody recognized me. I was a new guy!

My repackaging was entirely successful, it seemed, because everybody liked me. Even my Dad! And all my attributes were reinterpreted in this glowing new light!

I wasn't weird!

I was hilarious.

I wasn't wimpy!

I was gentle.

I wasn't brooding.

I was SEXY!

And maybe I was. Because I went from the romantic success rate of a leper, with an *overbite*, to having a girlfriend two grades ahead of me who drove a red sports car, vroom vroom.

I was king of the world.

And not since Fonzie had I learned a lesson so profound, so powerful and so utterly false.

Looks are everything.

Moving along.

So there I am, dating my future wife! And one of the things I love about her is that she has this wonderful sense of adventure! She's lived in Bolivia where she worked at a school for street kids, and she has all these friends in Nicaragua, where she did other amazing things, and do I want to go to Nicaragua with her? And yes, of course I do.

And at this point I have in my head a basic, post-secondary level, liberal theology thing going. I love the gays, obviously! Obviously!

Love hating on bigoted Christians, really gets my teen angst funny bone, just yummy, so fucking sweet!

But I still like capitalism pretty well, at this point. I mean, after all, I'm one of the ones who is going to *truly* make it, and I want to be free to do that.

Over thirty, living in Edmonton, I believed this.

I still believe this.

But I don't like war. Because . . . it's bad.

But I like freedom, and I heard on the news that war gives people freedom, so . . .

But then I go to Nicaragua. And Nicaragua bleeds politics. And then you know about how the Cold War was not a cold war. If you were in Vietnam or Afghanistan or Korea or Nicaragua, then it was a very hot, very long war, and in Nicaragua everybody I saw, my age or older, was all up in it. All of them lost friends, took lives, and all of them make a dollar a day, doctors make two dollars, cab drivers more than that. Because they might get some of my good white money.

And even though it's already so cheap, they got a special zone in the middle of the country. It's called the Zona Franca! And in that zone, you can hire people even cheaper. To work even longer. In even worse conditions. And so companies set up there. Companies from America, and Europe, and Canada.

And now I know how the world works, more than I did, and now I post stuff to Facebook, and annoy everybody, and it's actually because I am just sick to death about it. Sometimes I think I'd unknow it all. If I could.

The performer leans in confidentially.

And the way things are going these days, I mean . . .

The performer speaks loudly, as if he wants to be overheard.

I would like to review some of my positions! I now feel that Climate Science is not settled, and the crime bill was a . . . rrrr . . . *good* thing for Canada. Yeah, let's build those prisons, you know, unreported crime is way way up, and the Prime Minister himself has really good . . . hair.

So that is I think what they wanted me to say, and actually, it's a real load off, so —

We hear an offstage noise.

Did you hear that? Did you —

Long blackout. We hear the sounds of a scuffle.

No!

We hear the sound of a silenced shot. There is a long pause.

Moving along.

So I'm going out to Devon, little town just outside Edmonton, where my brother was killed in his car accident. This would be the two-year anniversary of his death. So, me and my family, we're doing that thing, you know? Where we get together, and we put a new cross out on the highway, and we talk a little about our grief and how much we love each other.

And then we go out to this dinner being thrown at the Legion. The dinner is being thrown by this prominent citizen of Devon, because his wife died of cancer one year ago today and she loved it when everybody got together and had dinner.

So my family and I end up spending a good chunk of our mourning ritual at somebody *else's* mourning ritual. And it's nice, on the one hand. It's nice that there are rituals, and people care enough to attend them, and people are remembered. But on the other hand, there's just so much grief. So much grief you have to . . . *stack it.*

And I'm driving home from the mourning, and this cop stops me on the highway. There's a major accident up ahead and I have to use a detour. I can't believe it.

Again.

Another.

More. More.

I sit in my car looking at the cop for too long. He doesn't know what's going on for me. Cleaning up pain is his whole job. And it wears on him. I can see it. Just behind his eyes.

And I don't know if he has a drink when he gets home, or rolls a joint, or prays until he feels lighter, or makes love until transcendence, or exercises until exertion blocks out his mind. But I bet he does something.

We all do something.

Besides . . .

Smoke a J and TV becomes engrossing.

Do some mushrooms and a walk through the park is *Lord of the Rings.*

Do some ecstasy and watermelon is orgasmic, and orgasms are indescribable.

Do a line of coke and be so smart, so fast, so on! Hold your own with anybody on earth! Discuss time with Einstein and impress him with your calculator watch! Sniff!

And yeah, sooner or later you get sick and tired of being sick and tired and you wonder about giving it all up. But for what?

What will you do instead?

Kingsley Amis said human life is so horrible that the only thing to do is what you want.

Frank Sinatra said he feels sorry for people who don't drink, because when they wake up, it's as good as they're gonna feel all day.

Dr. Dre said, "Hey hey. Hey hey. Smoke weed every day." But I don't think he's a real doctor, so . . .

In any case, the votes are in. And it seems nobody wants to spend all their time in *reality*. Not this reality, anyway.

Just a side note.

The performer flashes his backlight along with his speech.

Everybody's special. You're special. I'm special. Lemons are on special. Now and then, but given the choice, wouldn't you rather be really special, special to everybody. Hold a special place not just in the eyes of your child and in the bed of your lover but in the heart of your nation, in the imagination of a generation, in the mind of the world?

Me too.

Broken homes are not a lot of fun. You can ask Oprah if you don't believe me. But there is a privilege afforded children in this situation if they want it, and I did.

They get to switch parents.

The performer leans in confidentially.

You see, it was getting more and more crowded at my Mom's house. Jesus was taking up all this space! And he was constantly making my Mom do this crazy shit, like coming into my room and tearing down my Twisted Sister posters, and throwing out my Kiss tapes.

Plus my imagination was brimming with filthy things I'd never get to try since Mom kept a radio tag clipped to my ear and tracked me by satellite. I had to get outta there. I had to have my freedom.

I had to break my mother's heart.

So I did.

But I didn't have the courage to do anything directly so I just behaved worse and worse, and still worse, and even worse, and oh my goodness do you really want to behave that badly, *worse*.

Until my mother, exhausted from her full-time job, finally took me aside and said:

If you want to live with your father so badly, go. Just go.

So I went.

And that was how I learned at the tender age of thirteen the cowardly way to dump any woman. By simply behaving like such a complete asshole that the woman finally and bitterly thrusts you away from herself.

And I've used it many times since.

Moving along.

Dad's going to kill me for telling you this. This is what got me in all the trouble with the authorities last time. I feel close to you people. Fuck it. I want to tell you, I'm gonna tell you, I'll tell you, alright, here we go.

I am the son of *God*.

Yeah! It's no coincidence that I'm *Christ*opher. No. It's part of the divine plan. You see it's been a long time since I was here last. And since I'm here, it's like he's here too, right? 'Cause we're a trinity, right? The Father, the Son, the Holy Spirit. We're, like, three people, like, *entities* in one. Which is weird, let me tell you, but we cope.

And I try to do my job. Which is mostly to tell people to be nice to each other.

The performer singles out an audience member.

Come on, man.

And, to hang around with prostitutes. And later, when I'm thirty-three, which is –

He checks his watch.

– uh, *eight* years ago!

I have to die. For you. For all of you. I have to take the weight of your sins on my back, and die with them, so that you might be washed in the blood of the lamb –

That's me,

And be free to enter Heaven!

It's going to hurt, dying. I won't like it. But I don't expect any of you people are going to like it either. And it's no big deal for me. You know, because I know what's going to happen. You know, for me, when I see that bright light at the end of the tunnel, it's not like:

The performer becomes a man, dying.

JESUS CHRIST WHAT THE FUCK IS THAT?! OH MY GOD! IS THAT MY BODY DOWN THERE? OH, JESUS CHRIST! MY BODY MY FAMILY MY LIFE!

No for me it's more like:

Hey Dad.

So, you know, I'll die for you, and all, but don't sweat it. It's *easy*. It's easy to die, for a really good reason, and then go and sit on the right hand side of God, in Heaven, forever.

What's hard, what's hard — I imagine and I'll never know. What's hard is to die for no real reason, and then, not to know *what* happens next.

Jesus.

I don't know how you people do it.

Moving along.

By the time I was seventeen, I had already, sort of, been *around the block*.

I was heavily into celebration, over having recently become sort of acceptably good-looking. And I had just enough of whatever's required to occasionally catch a bad girl's eye. And I attempted this, whenever I could.

So anyway, one night, me and a buddy, we had had a few beers and we decided to do that low down dirty male teen thing. And tell the tales. Tickle the fancies! Dish the dirt and come clean.

Now, this is not as tasteless as you might expect. I mean, even in a drag-out session, men will generally confine themselves to:

The general quality, the personages involved, the location, if outlandish, the duration, if impressive, and, well, that's about it. There's a courtliness that even teens will observe, even when they don't have to, and details are considered to be *gauche*.

So, I'm shamefaced to say that I told every tale I had, but I told them *sparingly.*

I told the one about the . . .

Lifeguard at the waterpark, the recording booth at studio eighty-two, the one by the river, the many in the car, the ice cream, the strawberries, the older woman with a doughnut fetish, the singer with the ferret.

I told head and tail of every bad boy romp of my young life, sitting in that van, *right outside our house.* And I might be talking still except I heard:

The performer becomes his dad.

Jesus Christ, son! Will you shut the fuck up! I can hear every goddamned word that you're saying!

You see, Dad wanted me to be a good boy, and I was a little confused about that. I always kind of thought he'd sort of prefer it if I was a little bit bad, like he used to be. But that isn't what he wanted at all — in fact, that's what he was afraid of.

And he could have said something sooner, because it takes a Mack truck full of explanation to outweigh a tablespoon of example, and it was too late. I was already me!

And I hate who I am.

Oh, wait a second, I like who I am.

Wait a minute, I hate who I am.

No, no, I like it.

I mean, look at this stuff whoo. This is what I do. For a living.

Sorry. No, I shouldn't like this much, it's bad, right? Because of taxes! There's public money in this, so it's bad to like it too much. People don't like it. People don't like —

— artists.

Moving along.

Let me say in my defense that it was a very long day, I had flown across a border, I was exhausted, I was even a little *high*. I say all of this in my defense, and I need to, because I was about to commit a HYPOCRISY.

So I had flown back after spending a month in Atlanta, Georgia, far away from my beautiful wife, who I missed terribly, and in a sort of celebration of my homecoming the neighbour lady from across the street had taken it upon herself to arrange a special surprise for me, and fill my water feature with fish!

You see, I keep a little fountain thing, like pssssssh, as a source of water for the neighbourhood birds, because I'm a bird guy, and I put out various foods for various birds and they show up!

I get blue jays and nuthatches and downy woodpeckers, and chickadees — sparrows — and magpies —

Magpies, right? I mean. How do you — What do you do? You can't kill them. It's illegal. Legally you can trap them, but you could spend your whole life doing that, they're just too smart, they're Lex Luthor birds —

So anyway she had filled up my water feature with fish, goldfish, how delightful! Let's see how they're doing! Ohhh . . .

THEY'RE DEAD. They had jumped the gun, spring comes so late, later and later all the time, it was too cold and the fish are DEAD, and so my special surprise is, like, eighteen dead fish in my pond, so, okay, fine, we start to scoop them out, my suitcases are still sitting there in the yard, and I'm scooping corpses, and we line them up on the porch like a cult suicide.

And it's so depressing, and we wrap them up and throw them in the garbage, And then the neighbour lady appears, the neighbour lady who did it, she appears, with her daughters, her super-cute dewy-eyed daughters, and they wanna see the surprise! They want to see the fish! How are the fish doing? How are the fish doing?

And we have to say, well –

The performer speaks to the two young girls.

They're dead, they died, it was too cold, it was too cold and brrrrrr! They froze, the little fishies, and they're DEAD.

And their little eyes teared up, and their faces fell, right to the ground, and there was this moment, this horrible moment of silence, and it seemed like someone should say something, and I'm that guy, who says something when something needs to be said, so I said, I said to the girls –

The fish – are in Heaven.

And the mother looks at me like –

And my wife looks at me like –

And the kids look at me like I'm lying to them, because I am. And the awkward moment passes and we go on with our lives. And when they're gone, my wife says –

That was weird, dude.

Yeah. Yeah, it was.

Moving along.

So I am at the Vancouver aquarium. It's a great facility, full of amazing creatures, but I wanna see the humpback whales.

And I had somewhere a fact in my head, kind of a fake fact, jostled together with all the other facts, but I think I "know for a fact" that whales communicate not only with sounds, but with telepathy.

So I thought I would try it.

There was kind of a basement level downstairs where you could look into the tanks and there they were! These beautiful mammals, floating in a circle, their heads facing in, like they were sharing a joint.

I put my head against the glass and I start thinking into the tank. I set up a mantra, a simple message, a positive one — "I love you." I am thinking "I love you, I love you" into the tank, just thinking it over and over again, sort of imagining my thoughts traveling over to the whales in their smoking area . . .

And then, one of the whales hears me! One of the whales hears me, and disengages from the group. He comes over and floats right down, and we are face to face, and I am thinking "I love you," and we stay like that for about a minute, and then I just can't take it anymore and it's over.

I feel great! I am Dr. fucking Dolittle over here! And I join my friends at the walrus tank.

But that walrus hates me. He *hates* me.

He head butts the glass when I touch it, and it's me. My friends are trying stuff, nothing. Weird. So we go upstairs, but what we don't know is that the walrus's outdoor enclosure is right beside the stairs. So when this thing angrily bursts out of the water, I have to say, I was pretty scared. This thing is the size of a grizzly bear, and it burst out of the water with such force that his eight-hundred-pound body slid right at the limits of his wall, which put his tusks about a foot from my head. And he was making a walrus roar, like —

The performer roars like a walrus.

And I'll never know what that walrus was thinking. But sometimes I think that maybe he heard me. Heard me, somehow, and maybe he was thinking:

Well if you love us so much, why don't you get us the fuck outta here?

Moving along.

I remember my Uncle Nathan and my Aunt Nancy. Uncle Nathan was a party guy, you know, not a coke and strippers party guy, but a couple of beers and his family party guy. You know, he played all these instruments, and between us kids we played all these instruments. We'd get together with the whole family and we'd massacre these classic songs, like:

The performer sings while miming drums.

Lady Madonna, children at your breast.

Everyone would clap and laugh, and have a good time, and you'd feel that they were a part of something. You know, that's what Uncle Nathan and Aunt Nancy did for the family, along with everything else. They were the cheerleaders, they were the glue, they were the energy behind every big family outing. They just seemed to have enough joy and ambition to carry us all.

And I remember driving in the car with my Uncle Nathan. We were listening to a tape on the stereo, Billy Joel, *The Bridge,* I think the album was. And on that album there is a song about how Billy Joel doesn't need companionship. He doesn't need a wife, or even friends because what he has is a baby grand piano.

And I remember my Uncle Nathan being very excited about this song. I remember him trying –

– a bit desperately –

– to convince me of its arching truth and veracity, and I remember why. Because six months earlier, Aunt Nancy had died, after a long, long bout with cancer, and Uncle Nathan still had his piano.

It's a nice thought –

Maybe.

– that your stuff can replace your people? I mean, oftentimes you can keep your stuff if you love it enough, you can maintain your car, tune your piano, and upgrade your computer. People. Near as I can tell, too much love just makes them die quicker.

And every life that passes leaves behind a specific lesson, based on who that person was. But every life that passes also leaves behind the same lesson: That we too will one day die. That life is finite, and therefore precious.

Moving along.

In every life, people amass collections of things that strike their fancy, say: books of a certain author, or china plates with little bunnies on them, the pinky fingers of hitchhikers.

Me? I collect the things I did not say. See I'm a daydreamer by nature, and as a pastime, I like to think about times wherein a confrontation took place!

Or, much more often, *didn't* take place.

And I think about what I could have said to that person, and I say it. I'm fearless! I am rude and pithy! I have instantaneous perception of the unfair *mojo* being placed on me. And I tell it like it is.

Let's see, there's a few around I can show you. Oh, uh, oh, here, this one's pretty good. It's this:

You hurt me. It hurt. The way your relationship with God was always more important than your relationship with me.

And this one is good. It's common, though. I must have a million of these. It's common but it's good. It's one of those you know, common but it's good. It's this:

I QUIT! You pompous little prick! You can take this job and shove it right up your ass.

But this one is. I only have one of these. It's kind of my, you know, it's, it's this:

I love you, brother. And I didn't always understand what you wanted from us. What you wanted from the world. But, I love you. And I wish we had more.

This is my collection of things I did not say. And a collection is nothing if you don't show it to somebody now and again, so I thought I'd show it to you. This is my collection of things I did not say, all said. All said to all of you.

TAH-DAH!

Moving along.

Being Canadian, a thing we do is measure distance in time. For example:

Yeah, it's about three hours from Edmonton to Calgary.

Well, I have gone quite a distance now, in this jalopy I call a body, and in a blink of an eye, I have traveled eleven years from my brother's death. It's been twenty-seven years since I left my mother's home and twenty-two since I left my father's. These earth-shattering events are still visible when I look back at my personal horizon, but they shrink. Slowly, they get smaller.

The lessons of grief have kept my family together, though some of us more than other. This has been helped by the joy of babies. People having babies reminds us that this is a two-way deal. And while it is horrible that people go away, it's a miracle that new people also show up.

There are many ways to grieve entirely wrong offered by our feel-no-pain culture, and of all of them, only workaholism is good for your career. The drinking, drug abuse and promiscuity are not good news in most workplaces, but they are somewhat acceptable in show business. Which is probably why it is so attractive to guys like me.

Now that I'm happily married, all that seems so far away. And younger people sometimes ask me —

How do you know if someone is the one? And my answer is, you just do. It doesn't mean that there aren't problems, it doesn't mean everything is perfect, but there is a singular oneness about the one that leaps over everything and compels you to stay.

So if you're sitting around asking yourself —

Is he or she the *one?*

Maybe he or she isn't. Because the one will not be denied. It grabs you by your lapels and slaps your stupid face until you get it. It is an offer you cannot refuse.

And even though our lives are far from stable, it is our plan to make one of those babies. We've both done a lot of grieving, you know, and now, we want in on the miracle.

Moving along.

I was sitting in the men's room of a greasy spoon the other day. It was a less-than-charming place, believe you me, and I was about to dismiss it, you know, *aesthetically* but then I noticed this —

— hand painted tile on the wall.

And it was beautiful! And it was the only one like it in the room! And it occurred to me then, that I could go about and break every single tile in this place and maybe each one of them would be so —

Fabulously replaced!

And then this greasy spoon would have the most amazing men's room of any greasy spoon in Canada, possibly NORTH AMERICA!

But then I thought no. They wouldn't thank me for that. No one appreciates damage. At the time.

Moving along –

Just a side note –

For example –

Moving along

Moving along

Moving along

The performer struggles to say it.

Moving Along.

THE END

BONUS MATERIAL

[NOTE! This is not finished material, because it has not yet been performed. But since I last did Moving Along, my wife and I have been blessed with a baby boy, who is rock star cool. As such, when I speak of his arrival, it might go something like this . . .]

The Performer: So, Jania had heartburn. She had heartburn and she never gets heartburn and what could this mean? So she peed on a test. She came and showed me the test and we were really scared and we decided to go to the drugstore for another test.

And Jania was saying:

Just last weekend I was in Jasper. I was drinking and hot-tubbing in Jasper and those are the two things you are totally supposed to not do.

She said that, and there was fear, but also a crazy hope. A weird crazy hope that maybe life wouldn't change, and there would be a miscarriage and that would be sad, but maybe for the best because Jania is doing a project in Nicaragua and my movie is at Cannes and please God, we'll make our dreams come true if only we're not pregnant.

And all this is even though we were kind of trying. We did go off birth control and let's face it. We were doing it.

But we also had that chat, not that long ago. "Let's put it off another year," we said. "I'll go back on birth control," she said. But even while we were having that conversation, she was already pregnant.

And we still weirdly half-hoped that this would blow over. That we could not grow up for just a little while longer. But we were pregnant, of course, because those tests are crazy good. Even the cheap ones are simply never wrong.

And then we're pregnant. And Jania is sick all the time, and this does mean I have a designated driver, but she also wants to go home early all the time, so I never get to really drink, you know?

And we borrow a crib and a change table and oceans of hand-me-downs arrive, some for right away, and others for growing into, and the midwife and self-hypnosis, that will make the birth pleasant and easy through the power of our minds.

And people tell us how hard everything will be, and how we'll never have sex again, and never sleep again, never have fun again, and never look each other in the eye again, and we make the choice to believe none of them. And we live in hope and fear.

And then the day comes. Jania says:

We're having a baby.

And I think she means, like, in general, and I'm all like:

We sure are, baby!

And she says: No, like today.

And so we fly into action, and Jania breathes and listens to calm voices on her phone and I set up the pool and the hoses, and our friend the doula comes over, and our friend the acupuncturist, and we try like hell to have that baby at home, which is our right, as hippies.

But the midwife finally says no, and at the twenty-three-hour mark, it's time to go to the hospital.

But they're full! It's Alberta and it's an oil boom and everyone moved here and one tiny effect of that is the hospital is completely full, and even though we give in, we surrender, we will now accept drugs! It's only morphine and a triage bed for now, and "for now" means nine hours.

And we use our self-hypnosis to ease any leftover pain the morphine misses, because even though we asked, they won't give us anymore.

And then it's time for the epidural, which will take away all the pain below the waist and allow us to finally get that baby out. And it was hour thirty-eight.

They told us to sleep, because in two hours or so we're totally gonna have this baby, and I fall asleep in the fold-out armchair thing and Jania doesn't. Because, I don't know. Maybe she has a lot on her mind or something.

And then it's time. And wife is so tired, it's been so long, she's exhausted, and the boy is not co-operating. His head is down, but just a little to one side, cocked quizzically, as if to say:

Sorry about your vagina.

Though he has yet to actually apologize.

And he is a he, despite our oddly firm belief that it would be a girl. So many girl's names picked out for girls, and so few for boys. We had eschewed all superstition, but on this point we were utter believers in our gut feeling.

But back to the birth, because people, that shit is still going on! Now it's time for *interventions*.

First up! Suction.

I pictured it like a vacuum cleaner, some kind of hose attached, but no, it's a hand pump! Just pump, pump, pump, and the suction cup has the head, and the doctor pulls, and this doctor is this muscular lady and she like, *reefs* on this suction cup.

No dice.

Now it's time for forceps. And forceps are these David Cronenberg-looking ice cream scoops. Slip one side in and under his tiny head. Slip the other one in. Okay.

But then they cross over. And they link, and it's like this brutal robot that has fistfuls of my baby's skull. And the doctor's biceps flex, and that robot pulls out that head, and the rest tumbles forth.

And it's no cutting the cord for Dad. The NICU team is in, and he's under the lamps, and I run over there, and I'm screaming:

It's a boy! It's a boy!

Because I can't believe it's a boy, after believing it was a girl for so long, for absolutely no reason.

And his head is cut up, and it's the weirdest shape. But there he is. That's my boy. My son. And I insist that he be moved as soon as possible to Jania for skin-to-skin bonding, because as a hippie, it's all I have left. And I said:

You did it.

You did it.

DELETED SCENES

[NOTE: This is material that I found later to be less vital to the show compared to new things I wanted to bring in. I include them here as an extra, like Nick Fury showing up after the credits.]

THE MONSTER

The Performer: So I am just out of university and I am trying desperately not to waiter, as I have just done five years at Earl's and now hate the public.

Yes, I mean you.

So I am trying hard to get any kind of gig I can, basically all the time, and one of the gigs I could get was being a monkey. I had this leather ape mask that was really good, and I would put in on and be a monkey. So here it was New Year's Eve and there one of those First Night festivals, which makes no sense, because it's not the first night, it's the last night, the first night is tomorrow night, and there's no festival for that. Although —

I myself like to observe Hangover Day, a floating holiday which occurs on days which cannot always be predicted, up to one hundred per year.

So I'm being a monkey, jumping around in the terrarium lobby of this giant theatre complex, which I would later be hired at and fired from! And it's tiring, even though I am in my early twenties. It's a tiring job, and the only time I can rest is during my short rides in the glass elevator. So I am at ease, in my monkey mask, riding up this glass elevator and down below me, I see a kid in a stroller. He's maybe four years old and I see him, and I see him see me. He sees me and he's kind of scared, and I don't know why, I really can't explain, but I see the kid seeing me and I —

Makes a threatening gesture, becomes the kid being scared.

And I get out of the elevator and forget about it. And then a while later, I am in the glass elevator, and I look around, and the kid is there in the elevator with me. And I feel guilty, I don't want a scene, so I am just neutral, chilling, nice monkey, and the kid is terrified, just terrified to be in the elevator with the monster that threatened him earlier, and no one mentioned me or spoke to me and then the ride was over and we all got out.

And I think that kid thought — that monsters exist. That monsters exist and it's a secret. It's a secret and adults don't talk about them, just like they don't talk about lots of things, like sex or drugs or the vibrating cucumber in the bedside table. Monsters exist, and I know.

Because I was one.

THE BACHELOR PARTY

The Performer: My friend is getting married, and I've been asked to stand up at the ceremony. It's the first time such a request has been made of me. Except for when my father got remarried in the MASSIVE MISTAKE of 1985. I call it a mistake but that's not really fair. I mean, in truth, it was more of a PLANE CRASH! A PLANE CRASH of a marriage! I attribute it not only to human error, but also to the general shabbiness of the craft itself. My suspicions about the covenant notwithstanding, there is a ritual to attend and I aim to attend it.

First things first, The Bachelor Party. Now, this is not the event it once was, let me tell you. I mean, these are the aughts and times have changed. Nobody wants to be alcohol poisoned, shackled, tattooed, have half an eyebrow shaved off, and put on a bus to Tijuana with a stripper named *Jugsy* anymore.

Sad, but true.

We're planning the enlightened bachelor party, the twenty-first-century bachelor party, and here's the main thing: girls get to come. Not just girls, but the bride herself will be there. Frank Sinatra would bitchslap me for the bachelor party that I am planning. But the ritual needs to fit the humans it's designed for, and my friend is not a coke and strippers kinda guy. However, I'm getting him a stripper anyway. And here's the catch. It's okay for a woman to strip in front of other women at a private party, at a private home, *if* she's not really a woman in the first place.

So the stripper appears. A charming young man-lady — beautiful, really. The kind of drag queen that every straight man in the room wants immediately. I mean they know she's a man under there, but it doesn't matter. She's that hot. I screamed out an introduction and in she danced and danced and danced and danced and DANCED. A shoe flew off and she flailed her arms and turned on my ceiling fan. She danced and danced, and everybody screamed and clapped their hands and a glow seemed to rise out from her. And then everybody rose up off the ground, just a bit, just a few inches, just levitating above the ground. And then everyone turned into animals, a bit, just a little bit, just whiskers and claws, just protruding, just a few inches, a thin sheen of fur bristled deliciously on everybody and then it was over. The effects went away and yet they lingered.

Because it was a fucking good party.

PLAYOGRAPHY

SuperEd – 1996

Ha! (with Wes Borg) – 1997

Tranny Get Your Gun (with Darrin Hagen) – 1997

Indulgences – 1997

Little Orphan Tranny (with Darrin Hagen) – 1998

The Day Billy Lived – 1998

Wrecked – 1999

Men Are Stupid, Women Are Crazy (with Darrin Hagen) – 1999

On Being a Peon – 1999

Porn Star – 2000

Moving Along – 2000

The Critic (songs by Ron Pederson) – 2000

Do It Right – 2001

Blackbird Puppet Project (with The Green Fools) – 2001

Broken Horses, Broken Hearts (as Miles Cleveland) – 2001

The Monster Club (with Wes Borg) – 2001

Tranne of Green Gables (with Darrin Hagen) – 2002

DreamLife – 2003

Making Out (with Ian Rowe) – 2003

3...2...1 (with Nathan Cuckow) – 2003

BoyGroove (music by Aaron Macri) – 2004

Faithless (with Steve Pirot) – 2005

Summer of My Amazing Luck (based on the novel by Miriam Toews) – 2005

Billy (Aboriginal version of The Day Billy Lived – with De-Bah-Jeh-Muh-Jig Theatre) – 2006

Wrecked (Toronto version) – 2006

PopTart – 2007

BASH'd (with Nathan Cuckow, music by Aaron Macri) – 2007

The Incredible Speediness of Jamie Cavanaugh – 2009

The Velveteen Rabbit – 2010

PopTart (full length version) – 2011

Slaughter Camp (music by Sidney Ellis Gaskin, lyrics by Kevin Gillese) – 2011

Public Speaking – 2012

Apocalypse, A Period Piece (with Michelle Kennedy) – 2013

UPCOMING PROJECTS

Champion

Irma Voth (based on the novel by Miriam Toews)

CHRIS CRADDOCK is an Edmonton based Actor/Producer/Writer. His theatre work in Canada has been recognized with four Sterling Awards and two Dora Mavor Moore Awards, and his film *Turnbuckle* was nominated for two AMPIA Awards. He is the proud recipient of the Embridge Emerging Artist award, the Centennial Medal for his contribution to the Arts in Alberta, and the Alberta Book Award for his collection of plays for teens *Naked at School.* His musical *BASH'd* (co-written and performed with Nathan Cuckow) received a 2007 GLAAD media award for achievement in NYC Theatre. He is currently celebrating the airing of a new comedy series in which he served as lead actor and Head Writer, *Tiny Plastic Men* on SuperChannel.

Chris graduated from the University of Alberta's BFA Acting Program in the spring of 1996 and since then he has worked on stages, and in front of cameras, all across Canada.

Chris has created compelling and engaging works for a broad cross-section of audiences. His plays have been performed at the New Repertory Theatre in Boston, The Zipper Theatre in NYC, Celebration Theatre in Los Angeles, Calgary's Sage Theatre and High Performance Rodeo, The Magnetic North Festival, Vancouver Comedy Festival, Edmonton Comedy Festival, SaskNative Theatre, International Fringe festivals in Montreal, Toronto, Winnipeg, Vancouver, Saskatoon, Toronto, NYC, and Orlando. He performed off-Broadway in his award-winning musical *BASH'd!*

He is the screenwriter of the bilingual feature film, *The Pharmacist/La Pharmacien,* winner of Best Feature at the Nevada Film Festival. Chris was the 2010 Writer in Residence at the Edmonton Public Library, and is currently writing for the CBC Radio's *The Irrelevant Show,* and finishing his second season of *Tiny Plastic Men* which has been nominated for a Canadian Screen Award for Best Comedy Series.